Hizmet Movement, a Lived Experience, and Introspections on Pedagogy

Koray Lynx

Hizmet Movement, a Lived Experience, and Introspections on Pedagogy

PETER LANG
New York - Berlin - Bruxelles - Chennai - Lausanne - Oxford

Library of Congress Cataloging-in-Publication Data

Names: Lynx, Koray, author.
Title: Hizmet movement, a lived experience, and introspections on pedagogy / Koray Lynx.
Description: New York, NY: Peter Lang, 2024. | Includes bibliographical references.
Identifiers: LCCN 2023046990 (print) | LCCN 2023046991 (ebook) | ISBN 9781636674636 (paperback) | ISBN 9781636674681 (pdf) | ISBN 9781636674698 (epub)
Subjects: LCSH: Education–Turkey–Philosophy. | Gülen Hizmet Movement. | Gülen, Fethullah–Teachings. | Critical pedagogy–Turkey. | Education–United States–Philosophy.
Classification: LCC LA941.8. L96 2024 (print) | LCC LA941.8 (ebook) | DDC 370.9561–dc23/eng/20231103
LC record available at https://lccn.loc.gov/2023046990
LC ebook record available at https://lccn.loc.gov/2023046991

DOI 10.3726/ b21458

Bibliographic information published by the Deutsche Nationalbibliothek.
The German National Library lists this publication in the German
National Bibliography; detailed bibliographic data is available
on the Internet at http://dnb.d-nb.de.

Cover design by Peter Lang Group AG

ISBN 9781636674636 (paperback)
ISBN 9781636674681 (ebook)
ISBN 9781636674698 (epub)
DOI 10.3726/b21458

© 2024 Peter Lang Group AG, Lausanne
Published by Peter Lang Publishing Inc., New York, USA
info@peterlang.com—www.peterlang.com

All rights reserved.
All parts of this publication are protected by copyright.
Any utilization outside the strict limits of the copyright law, without the permission of the publisher, is forbidden and liable to prosecution.
This applies in particular to reproductions, translations, microfilming, and storage and processing in electronic retrieval systems.

This publication has been peer reviewed.

FOREWORD

I have had the pleasure and opportunity to work with doctoral students and form life-long relationships. In so doing, I have learned a great deal about each person's journey as a scholar. Dr. Koray Lynx (formerly Yusuf İncetaş) and I have known each other for nearly over twenty years, and I continue to learn from and about him as a person and scholar. We have had many long talks about education, life, religion, and progress; and while we do not always agree, he always has been gracious and generous to a fault. In many ways we are very different people: I come to this task as an outsider: someone born in the US who identifies as Black, Christian, female, monolingual, and straight. In some ways we are very similar people, holding high personal standards, sharing what we know with others, and being available to support people on their life and educational journeys.

The scholarship in this book does not disappoint: It expands our knowledge and understanding beyond Western philosophies and theories about education and pedagogy. Dr. Lynx provides insights that are richly complex and textured as he brings a unique one-of-a-kind perspective to his scholarship. His perspective provides the reader with an authentic and thick description of his positionality, a history of the *Hizmet Movement* (HM) or Service Movement, an explication of Fethullah Gülen's writings, as well as a coveted personal interview of his philosophy of education. Dr. Lynx shares authentic and important background knowledge needed by readers unfamiliar with Islam, Fethullah Gülen's philosophy of education, the socio-political history of Turkey, and the history of Turkey's educational system, especially the HM.

An outstanding feature of Dr. Lynx's discussion of his positionality is his willingness to share his vulnerabilities. His narrative turns the idea of an objective observer on its head since a detached objective observer/researcher does not exist. Every researcher enters research with life experiences, lived within a culture, a gender, a language, and for some a religion. As such, every researcher brings ideological and theoretical perspectives with them to the process, failing to explicate perspectives honestly and openly does not mean they do not exist. In fact, it is a short-sighted, illogical, and a Westernized idea to pretend researchers are dispassionate observers devoid of biases, empathy, opinions, and prejudices. In this book, we come to understand that Dr. Lynx brings life experiences that permit him to be a thoughtful observer of HM schools as someone who is intimately knowledgeable. As a Turkish man who is a former HM student and teacher, he can observe and understand HM school contexts in ways that few other researchers can, possessing insider knowledge (cultural, linguistic, and religious). He also shares retrospectively, that his close ties to HM at times were an obstacle as he wanted to provide an accurate account and wondered if his emotional, financial, and philosophical attachment would affect how and what he observed and understood about HM education. Importantly, he understands HM's goals, philosophy, and religious connections adding incontestable knowledge to his phenomenological study. His personal narrative also supports readers' understanding of how he has framed this book by relaying a brief narrative of his life experiences within a pithy overview of the HM. His chronological retelling of the HM focuses on economic, educational, social, political, and religious changes in the movement from the 1920s to 2016. Woven throughout the historical review are discussions of the influence of Mr. Fethullah Gülen.

Dr. Lynx begins relying upon how his life experiences, broad knowledge base, and scholarship inform this study, while simultaneously describing his personal journal within the HM. Few scholars bring such first-hand understanding to their research or the ability to meld authentic cultural, linguistic, and Islamic religious knowledge and apply Western notions of conducting research. Dr. Lynx's early school experiences as a bicultural/bilingual child within a colonialized system are hard to read, yet after years of school-based trauma, he is introduced to HM by a neighbor. In many ways, HM saved his life; his early experiences within HM were a time of growth and wonder. These experiences included his attending Maltepe Dershanesi, an HM institution, and acceptance into the teacher preparation (with a focus on English as a second language) at Selçuk University. As a college student, he became more invested in HM, from listening to the founders and promoters of HM to selling subscriptions to HM publications. Dr. Lynx also openly shares his coming-of-age, battle with depression, closeted homosexuality, and the inner struggle between his Islamic beliefs and training under HM, with awareness of sexuality. He also brings extensive teaching experience as he taught for two decades in the HM system, teaching English as a second language, and traveling throughout Central Asia and Indonesia. His experiences make possible his rich cultural, educational, linguistic, pedagogical, philosophical, religious, and theoretical knowledge to later discussions of pedagogy and teaching. After immigrating to the US, he explains how HM charter schools were established under the No Child Left Behind act and as they have continued to function.

While media outlets throughout the US openly complained about their inability to contact and interview Mr. Fethullah Gülen, Dr. Lynx drew on his HM contacts to arrange an interview in a few days! He traveled to Mr. Gülen's compound and waited patiently for an opportunity to conduct an interview, parts of which are in this book. With this broad background, Dr. Lynx's study in select HM schools in different US geographical spaces noted curricular, gendered, linguistic, pedagogical, and political structures. He interviewed eight other Turkish male HM educators, five of whom are included in this book. His description of his findings, discussion, and recommendations offers the reader a glimpse of the work of HM schools in the USA. Readers will gain an appreciation for an alternative approach to educational pedagogy, one that is supportive of academic and personal growth and connectedness among people. Dr. Lynx concludes with recommendations for HM that include improving teacher education and broadening the HM curriculum and philosophy.

Arlette Ingram Willis
Champaign, IL

CONTENTS

	Introduction	1
Chapter 1	The Lived Experience	3
Chapter 2	The History	27
Chapter 3	The Philosophy	53
Chapter 4	The Pedagogy and The Interviews	63
	Appendix A	89
	References	103

INTRODUCTION

In this book, I set out to reflect my lived experience within the Hizmet Movement (HM) from a phenomenological viewpoint. I detail the transformation of HM along with my own transformation over a span of three decades. This book does not shy away from sensitive subjects such as LGBTQA+ topics in this Turkey-based, Muslim educational movement. Through a process that took over five years to complete through an arduous interview process with Mr. Gülen and extensive literature review of his writings, I detail Gülen's life, a short history of the Turkish Republic, and Gülenian philosophy on education. A full copy of the interview with Mr. Fethullah Gülen on education and language is available at the end of the book.

Chapter 1 locates my own initial foray into the HM as a youth in Turkey during the 1980s, contextualizing my lived experience as a college student and secondary school educator for two decades within its larger history. This chapter interweaves research literature and autoethnographic data into a bricolage account to illustrate logistical, motivational, and philosophical dynamisms associated with Hizmet schools in Turkey, Uzbekistan, Indonesia.

Chapter 2 includes an historical-political, cultural-historical background of HM and Mr. Gülen's life. The linear order of the chapter starts with the early roots of the New Turkish Republic during the 1920s; the ontogenesis of

Fethullah Gülen into the leader of the movement in the 1940s and 1950s; the birth of HM during the 1960s; and its evolution from a national, communal entity into a global institution into the new millennium.

Chapter 3 explores the Gülenian Philosophy on Education and the HM schools. While the chapter relates Gülen's thoughts on his educational philosophy from our interview in Spring of 2011, the final corpus of the content presented was shaped as a collaborative account. Indeed, in order to conduct the interview, I agreed to honor a few conditions when cultivating the fruit of our exchange. As such, the passages relating to our conversation were derived from a compilation of my own initial interview notes; the correction and expansion of these comments by a trusted colleague of Gülen; direct verbal quotations from our conversation; and excerpts derived from his many writings.

Chapter 4 presents my interviews with eight HM educators and administrators. The chapter provides a series of ethnographic portraits that describe the site, individual, and beliefs of key personnel interviewed across several months. The portraits highlight both unique and common themes from each pedagogical constituent in relationship to the interviewees' perceptions on Gülenian philosophy and education. Direct statements from the interviews are those associated firsthand with the themes. Readers will note that the number of these items varied across conversations. These ethnographic accounts can be considered "qualitative pathways" that reflect the interviewees' perceptions of Gülenian educational philosophy.

The Recommendations and Conclusions chapter includes recommendations for HM and final thoughts on what has been presented in this book.

· 1 ·

THE LIVED EXPERIENCE

The Author

Coming of Age with the HM

I was born in the early 1970s in the northern German city of Hamburg when the *Hizmet Movement* or the Service Movement, which is the focus of the book, was barely flourishing and establishing lighthouses in a politically unstable Turkey.

HM started off as a small, private, focused *cemaat*, or community, and organically transformed into a large, global, organic, ideological entity over time. For the most part, the general literature refers to the initiative as the Gülen Movement; however, at my first introduction to this community and, during consequent interactions, every participant used the word "Hizmet". Hizmet is a Turkish word for "service". Because the larger purpose of the entity was to conduct altruistic actions and gain God's approval, participants highly refrained from the term "the Gülen Movement". Indeed, Gülen himself states that the HM "does not have a head or a chain of command; it is not organized, neither does it have any recruits. You just talk to people, it makes sense to them, and they light a torch wherever they themselves are" (personal interview). The HM is free and open to all. Initially, this philosophy made me admire the movement.

The Beginning

After World War II, Germany was defeated and lost most of its manpower to war. In order to bring the economy back on track, the German state sent recruiters to countries such as Spain, Italy, Greece, and Turkey to find blue-collar laborers to work in its coal and steel industry. They also regarded China as an option; however, because of logistical barriers and fears of xenophobia, that was shelved.

Those blue-collar workers came to be known as *Gastarbeiter* or guest workers. My parents were among the first *Gastarbeiters*; they met each other there. They had two boys—my older brother and me. My brother and I could not have been any more different; he was an outgoing, soccer-playing, trouble-making child and I was the stay-home, Barbie-loving, book-reading sissy boy. After my parents' failed attempt to send me to Turkey for my 1st grade and put me in a private boarding school, I came back to Germany. I started elementary school again in Hamburg and loved it. It was fun and I was learning a lot. Or so I had thought. As I progressed from first to second, and from second to third grade, I remember joyfully reading colorful storybooks and falling behind my peers because I needed more time and scaffolding to process the content. While my native German-speaking peers were on their fourth and fifth books, I remember trying hard to get to the end of my first. It did not make sense; I did not understand why I was behind even though I loved what I was doing. My parents talked to my teacher and the teacher just shrugged it off and asked me to make more effort and socialize with my German peers.

I tried exactly as asked and it did not work out. My mother hired a tutor, and I tried my best. I made some progress with my classes, but it was not enough. When I thought I was caught up, the class had already moved on to another subject. There was no win. I also made an effort to befriend German friends. It did not go well. I eventually became friends with a German girl who was a student with special needs. No one had wanted to make friends with her and I, so we became each other's friend. I also made an effort to befriend more German students from my class. I clearly remember one day at recess, some students from my class played some sort of catch. I mustered up my courage and joined in. The first person caught was a boy from our class and he was punished with kisses from the girls. When it was my turn and I was caught, they stuffed snow down my neck into my sweater. The message was clear.

My mental and emotional state started to decline after that, and I withdrew. I was failing in school, almost no one wanted to become friends with me, and misery was a constant friend. On that note, I have a class picture that was probably taken in 2nd grade. The picture was black and white, and I was sitting by myself on one side of the bench while the rest of the class had gathered on the other side. I wonder what my teacher may have thought when she saw the picture. My grown-up self now tells me that the picture showed my powerlessness against Western authority and my perception in their eyes as an outsider. As Said (1995) states,

> There are Westerners, and there are Orientals. The former dominate; the latter must be dominated, which usually means having their land occupied, their internal affairs rigidly controlled, their blood and treasure put at the disposal of one or another Western power. (p. 44)

The German school system was not equipped to address the needs of students with a different home language and culture. There was no concept of bilingual education, and I attended a school based on a sink-or-swim system. I needed academic support in my home language; however, the German education system was, and probably still is, ignorant of such a need. No one at school seemed to be concerned with my academics. In addition, my big brother was sent to an alternative school because he was very "active." The school system had already made a decision on our behalf and had set us up for failure because we were different. We were not allowed to flourish. Today, this reminds me of a Karl Marx (The Eighteenth Brumaire, n.d.) quote:

> They cannot represent themselves, they must be represented. Their representative must at the same time appear as their master, as an authority over them, an unlimited governmental power which protects them from the other classes and sends them rain and sunshine from above. (para. 15).

The Return to Misery

My parents were worried about our well-being and decided that they would give schooling in Turkey another shot.

Things did not improve there, either.

I was now in fourth grade. The school system was based on rote memorization, and I did not do well. We ended up residing with our abusive uncle and his neurotic wife. I was constantly scared because he looked for any excuse to beat us. My brother, who was in fifth grade, wanted to run away. That was a long year.

In the meantime, the German economy picked up and the German government did not need as many Turkish laborers. They offered incentives to Turkish guest workers under the condition these foreign workers would permanently return to their homeland. They were not allowed to come back. My parents, both with limited literacy skills, bought into that small incentive. After a lot of family drama and moving around Turkey to find a place to settle, my parents returned to our ancestral village which felt like the far end of the universe. After getting the lay of the land, I realized that my previous life in a big city was over. I was locked up in a god-forsaken place that was cold, poor, far from everything, and had no appeal to a teenager. I felt desperate; there was no light at the end of the tunnel. I still have nightmares about it to this day. My father, however, was a happy camper; his dreams had come true, and he wanted to live there forever. He wanted me to become the village shepherd. My mother and I, however, were used to city life. Inevitably, conflicts arose. We lived two hours from the closest major city. The miserable life became even more miserable, and soon after turned into bankruptcy.

When I attended school in Germany, my distinct, olive skin set me apart from other white students and prevented me from making friends. Now, in middle and high school, despite being in my native land, I was still quite different from the others: I spoke Turkish with an accent. I dressed differently, walked differently, talked differently. I listened to pop music in English and German, watched American movies when I could find them, and played games that were different from my peers. People perceived my character as being feminine and soft. My life experiences in Hamburg had been different compared to my peers' childhoods, who came of age in my ancestors/grandfather's small, isolated, rural hamlet. Hence, my age mates and I did not have much in common. I became detached, feeling awkward and uneasy to be "me" around others. On many occasions, both my peers and my teachers ridiculed me. I was alienated and lonely. Because we lived in a village far from the small town where the school was, I walked two miles every weekday, each way. During the trek, I remember trying to remain distant from other youths in the village: walking alone allowed me to dream of a friendly, familiar, comforting place where I felt at home. The walk gave me a chance to mentally go to a place where I *was* actually home.

In the meantime, my father had used up all his savings to build his dream house in the village, but now he had to work to feed his family. There were no job prospects. So, we moved. We moved a lot. I ended up attending so many different schools that I do not even remember how many today. As a result of the entire move and so many changes, I went through trauma that later turned into chronic depression. My middle school years and freshman year in high school were a blur; I had created an alternative universe in my mind as a coping mechanism and was preoccupied with it most of the time. There was no other way for me to deal with this truly existential crisis. I longed for my room in the Falkenried neighborhood in Hamburg, Germany.

Moving Forward

Fortunately, my family moved to another rural, but larger, town called Çankırı. It was a mid-size town by Turkish standards of 40,000 people, located two hours northwest of the capital city of Ankara. It was not Hamburg, but it was slightly better than village life. It was 1988, and my junior year of high school. It was during this year that I became acquainted with the Hizmet Movement (HM) circle through my next-door neighbor, who later became my classmate. He took me to an *Işıkevi* or lighthouse, a meeting place, and introduced me to *abis* or elder brothers.

A typical *Işıkevi* or lighthouse was basically an apartment rented by college students. They utilized this as a place to live, pray, refrain from sin, build brotherhood ties with each other, and welcome newcomers like me. The physical space consisted of a simple, clean apartment where male college students resided. The first visit I remember was filled with curiosity. I wondered if there was a catch. Mentally, I kept asking myself, "What am I doing here? Who are these people? What do they want from me? Why are they offering free food to me? And when are we going back home?" The answers to those questions were many years away, and for the time being, I was a little uncomfortable.

I was initially invited to lunches and dinners with the *abis* or elder brothers who were practicing Muslims and college students at public universities. In Çankırı city, there was not much to do: we would wander the streets aimlessly in the evenings. There was nothing better or worse to do. The town was so poor that it did not even have a gang! Yet, it was cold, and visiting the *abis* was the only other option. We read interesting books and did our homework.

I was failing in high school and any help was deeply appreciated. I still failed high school; however, I felt better spiritually and was able to get into college, as a result.

At home, I always endured a constant sense of dread and misery. We were poor, my mother was unhappy, my father was constantly trying to find work as a handyman, and my brother's teenage hormones were making him do all kinds of "teenager things." True to its name, the lighthouse offered uncomplicated simplicity and contentment. Spending time among the *abis* was the highlight of my day. I now felt comfortable with those people around me; they did not "pick on" my differences, did not take advantage of me, and were very kind. They taught us the importance of morals, good character, faith, and the basics of Islam.

Although my parents were Muslims, I had barely received any religious education up until I met the elder brothers, who were mainly in their 20s and attended college. Yes, we would observe religious holidays such as Ramadan and would occasionally go to the mosque for Friday prayers. However, we would also dine on pork sausage sticks—that my mother thought was beef—and celebrate Christmas with advent calendars. From the time I was 17 until 21, through the HM lighthouses I learned what it meant to be a Muslim. During subsequent visits in an age of suspicion and distrust, I was especially surprised at how easily these brothers would let me into their homes and lives with no personal or political agenda.

The *abis* or elder brothers also responded to questions we had about religion and pointed us in the right direction. I remember feeling relieved when I went to visit them each time. The atmosphere was somewhat mystical; it felt amazing. Perhaps it was because I was away from home and all the problems it was nesting seemed to be on hold. To put it in a very cliché way, it was like "breaking free". In time, I heard about HM's Zaman Daily newspaper, which sold only 3,000 copies per day back then (in its heyday, it sold over 900,000 print copies a day). Their headquarters was in Istanbul, but they also had offices across the country, including a very small office downtown Çankırı. I loved the downtown area with its artificial crowds during the day and glittering lights at night. It was especially fun in the summer, and I did not want to go home. I made friends with folks over there at the Zaman Daily office. It was exciting to hear news from the media, follow newspaper subscription numbers, and just mingle with the folks over there. I felt connected to the world and this gave me hope to go and live in a better place one day.

On that note, it is worthwhile pointing out that these HM lighthouses were somewhat private, but not secret places. During the 2000s, some individuals claimed the HM was opaque and did not reveal much to the outside world about how the movement functioned internally. This is true when one examines the HM from a liberal, Western, and contemporary lens in a country where you can exercise freedom of speech. However, in Turkey during my adolescence and young adulthood in the 1980s and 1990s, I witnessed first-hand the century-old, ultra-secular Kemalist oppression against religious groups. To some extent, this secular influence justified HM's opacity. For example, during the Kemalist era, a military cadet I knew reported he and his peers could not profess their piety in the military academy and were persecuted for doing so. One former cadet who was discharged from the academy toward the end of his last year was forced to pay the expenses he incurred while in school back to the Turkish state. This was an age when the Turkish military forced a legitimately elected government to step down, known as the 28 February Memorandum of 1997. Public institutions and higher education were highly regulated, and females were banned from wearing the hijab or the veil in those places and resorted to wearing wigs to cover their hair to comply with their faith.

To this day, I consider these practices as being Islamophobic as well as sexist. While males of the same religious groups walked around on campus freely, females were persecuted on their behalf. The hijabi female students were assigned to *ikna odaları* or persuasion rooms to take their headcovers off. Some professors would mark them absent even when they were physically present in class because of their headcovers. Some other faculty would refuse to lecture. This would not happen to their male counterparts. In short, during the ultra-secular Kemalist era, individuals seeking community experienced risks when getting involved with a religious group. This may have created an impression that the HM was opaque. Yet, I went in, I saw, and I became.

The College Student

College—Here I Come

Toward the end of my junior year at Çankırı High in 1989, my classmate and next-door neighbor, who had introduced me to HM, asked me what I thought about going to college. I was constantly failing in school in all subjects except English and Physical Education, and I did not ever think I would ever be able to get into college. My father wanted me to be a shepherd, and my mother, although she had the best intentions in her heart, did not have the social capital to guide me. She was spending her days in self-pity. Therefore, I did not bother responding to my friend's question. I longed for college, but I dropped the subject. However, my dear friend did not. The HM did not. Little did I know that my friend and elder HM brothers were working out a plan for me. Looking back now, I believe that at that exact moment, the universe came together and saw my state as a prayer and granted me my wish: a college education and freedom to explore the world. I could not have been happier about this potential opportunity.

Close to the start of my senior year in the Fall of 1989, my friend told me that there was a college prep course in the capital city of Ankara, which was a two-hour train ride away; Maltepe Dershanesi. These types of weekend cram schools were quite common in those days. If you wanted to go to any college in Turkey, you had to pass two centralized exams conducted by the Higher Education Council of Turkey. They were both around three hours long. The state schools did not prepare students to pass them (but claimed that their curriculum did), and the tests were designed to eliminate you, not to place you in college. The competition was tough; there were more than one million test-takers at the time, but only around 100,000 places available. If you wanted to get into an ivy league college, the chances were even slimmer, at around 10,000.

Maltepe Dershanesi was a blessing. It was an HM institution, so they gave us a heavily reduced rate, and provided overnight stays for free. We would catch the Çankırı-Ankara train right after school was out for the weekend on Friday afternoon and spend Friday and Saturday evenings at an HM dorm for the boys in Ankara. We would learn academic content and solve tests on Saturdays and Sundays at the dershane, and then catch the train back home on Sunday afternoon. This opportunity presented by the HM brothers was a true act of altruism; they really did not expect anything in return. There were people who were given the same opportunity but left the HM circle after they got into college. In a way, this overlapped with the HM philosophy. During my interview, Mr. Gülen stated that "you have a service, a form of "market of consent," which solely depends on the voluntary contribution of people with no center, organized structure, by-laws, officiality, and neither need one" (Personal Interview). Hence, whether or not people who benefited from HM services helped you back was a minuscule detail. HM's hope was that these young college prospects considered paying it forward on their own accord.

HM's Maltepe Dershanesi and other HM educational institutions fulfilled one very important mission by doing what they did: They mobilized underserved populations, e.g., students coming from economically disadvantaged households, girls, Kurds, and Arabs, and elevated them from working class to the middle, and upper-middle classes. For example, the southeast part of Turkey has been historically conservative and has been regarded as unsafe because of terrorism. Girls are not sent to school and child marriages are not uncommon. Terrorist groups also recruit male school-age children and force them up to the mountains. The HM changed this misfortune. They opened *okuma odaları* or reading rooms, basically cram schools for college preparation, and supported these underserved populations free of charge. In sum, what American capitalism did for baby boomers, HM did for underserved and vulnerable populations in Turkey.

At the end of my senior year in 1990, I failed all my classes again, except English and PE. I took make-up exams and failed again. Then, it finally happened: I gained entrance to Selçuk University's Teacher Prep program with a major in English as a second language in Konya, Turkey. I also qualified for a state grant. I remember opening the admissions letter. It was a surreal moment. I thought this was my ticket out of poverty, depression, and family drama. But there was one problem; I had failed my make-up exams in high school. However, placing students in college was a matter of prestige for high schools back then and they let me go. Konya was going to become my home for the next four years. It was five hours away from home and I thought that the farther I would go, the better it would be for my sanity. I got on the bus and did not look back.

I set out for Konya in the fall of 1990. Upon arrival, I was given an address to an HM dorm and, after a short wait, was assigned to a lighthouse by the district imam. It was walking distance away from my school. I was given a needs list that included a simple bed, mattress, bed sheets, pillow, a table, chair, and toiletries. With the little money I had, I went to get the items from the city. I had a roommate as well; it was a typical college lifestyle, mostly. We paid a fixed rate for rent and for meals. The house imam, who oversaw budgeting and management, would collect the rent money and give it to the district imam. The rent was pooled to ensure it paid for all the lighthouses in the district. Since each place had a different rent rate, those who were paying less rent supported those who were paying more. The meal money, however, was kept in the house and was spent carefully until the end of the month. The place I stayed was a three-and-a-half-bedroom house sitting in the middle of high-rise apartments. Each room slept two people. We had a house imam who oversaw the house affairs, mentored the newcomers, woke us up for prayers, managed the list for daily kitchen duty, and maintained communication with the HM higher-ups. We were all males and practiced conservative Islamic and Hizmet values.

Daily Routine in a Lighthouse

The daily routine revolved around prayer times. There were five times we prayed in a day. Morning prayer was before dusk. We conducted most prayers in the big room together, then the imam would read religious books and discuss matters related to Islam to enrich our knowledge. After that, there was a break. A small breakfast followed on the floor since dining tables were not part of the lifestyle. We did not have our own plates, either. But we had our own spoons! Everyone ate from the same large plate or bowl in the middle. Then we would go to school and come back for lunch and for noon prayer, the second prayer of the day. The campus was a ten-minute walk away, so this schedule worked because of the close proximity. We would go back to campus for afternoon classes and return directly home after. We would conduct the third prayer of the day, and then those who were on kitchen duty that day would get busy preparing dinner. Others would read, study, or just hang out. I was completely drawn into my studies. As my roommates would say, I was a Shakird (a general word for "student," also a word Bediuzzaman Said Nursi, the forefather of HM, used for his disciples). I would spend my time doing grammar exercises and reading English books. I did not talk to girls, nor was I interested. My homosexuality kept me away from them, and my internalized homophobia kept me away from my own homosexuality, at least for the time being. Overall, I was happy with the way I lived. Yet, differences between roommates surfaced from time to time.

After the evening prayer, the fourth prayer of the day, dinner was served. The last prayer was late at night, which people preferred to do on their own at times. There was no TV, and audio equipment was used only to listen to Mr. Gülen's taped sermons. Those who had the budget for it would watch movies in the movie theater or do other things for entertainment, without telling anyone, of course. It was the early 1990s, when wearing jeans was frowned upon, and playing music aloud in the house was not well received.

What we had learned in school we needed to pay forward. So, I taught English to middle school students, sold subscriptions for the *Sızıntı* or Fountain magazine (HM's monthly spiritual periodical), and found new subscribers for Zaman Daily. It was there and then that I started to become truly affiliated with HM. I prayed five times a day, read the Zaman Daily and the *Sızıntı* magazine, and attended the *sohbets* (talks on religious matters conducted in small circles of five to ten people). All this gave me a sense of peace and belonging. I learned who Hocaefendi (Mr. Gülen) was, read his books, and listened using a cassette player to his taped sermons given in mosques. I also started reading the *Risale-i Nur* or Epistles of Light, a collection of religious books by Said Nursi, the forefather of the movement. His books were difficult to understand, yet I liked the challenge, and it expanded my archaic Turkish vocabulary considerably over time. It was a simple and humbling lifestyle. We did not have much money and food was scarce. Yet, none of that really mattered. We were young and enthusiastic individuals excited to be part of something larger.

The Kamps

During my first winter break, instead of going home right away, I stayed behind and joined the *Kamp*. This was the name of a spiritual retreat time spent in other lighthouses or HM dormitories over winter break and summertime. It served to support the spiritual well-being of college students and to protect them from the potential immoral influences of the outside world. In other words, it was mental and spiritual cleansing. Participation in this program was voluntary, but "highly" encouraged. The content was strictly on morality, ethics, and faith and concentrated on disciplining the self to become a better individual. It was an inner jihad. There were no politics, no extremist ideas, or other imposed dogmas that could inflict hate toward others.

At first, I thought Kamp was a waste of time. I did not know what to expect. I soon found out that a day there would start with the morning prayer just before dawn, and then we would have a short reading of the *ilmihal* or the Muslim book of the catechism until sunrise. It was *mekruh*, or unfavorable, to sleep during sunrise since this was believed to take away from one's productivity. I did not like getting up early to prepare for prayers with cold water. It was especially chilly in the winter. Winters are brutal in Anatolia and there was no central heating. After the *ilmihal* lesson, we would have a break until breakfast, which people usually used to catch up with sleep. After breakfast, a two-hour silent reading followed. I fell asleep a lot during that reading time. Sometimes dozing off like that felt like the best sleep ever. My friends would make fun of me afterward. I am grateful to this day that we did not have cellphones back then lest they took my picture! Next, there would be the midday prayer followed by lunch. After lunch, we would listen to Mr. Gülen's tape-recorded sermons until the afternoon prayer. Then, another silent reading would take place (and another doze off!). The final events of the day would be the evening prayer, dinner, a G-rated movie, and the night prayer. The lights were out by 10:00 p.m. The *Kamps* were like applications of faith in Hizmet lighthouses on a regular day, except that these were more concentrated within a shorter timeframe. It was beneficial, but I still looked forward to getting to the last day. This was how my first year in college went in 1990–1991. Although most of these practices were greatly followed in subsequent years, things changed for me. HM was expanding, evolving, and changing rapidly.

So was I.

By the time I graduated from college, I was wearing jeans, going to the movies, skipping my daily prayers, eating out, listening to music on my double-bass stereo Walkman, and hanging out with female friends. I was also in a secret homosexual relationship and dealing with internalized homophobia—a homosexual individual's belief that homosexuality is wrong.

A Solid Realization

The concept of *change* in HM was prevalent back then. It was synonymous with revitalization. That meant you would change/move to a different house each year. There was also no confrontation or unwillingness from the brothers since obedience was a virtue. Like the rest of my roommates, I moved to another lighthouse in my second year. It was closer to school, so the commute to campus was shorter. This was my sophomore year in college, which meant I was going to move two more times in the future for my junior and senior years. I met the house imam and the rest of my new roommates. The house imam was a very knowledgeable individual studying theology. It seemed like he knew way more than others did. I later thought that was because he spent literally all his nights reading. The brothers in this apartment, on the other hand, were slightly better off financially than the ones in my previous house. When they went home for the break, they would always come back with extra food and supplies to share with us. This was a smaller apartment, so there were fewer of us. The living room also had an aquarium and many plants that my previous place did not. It was a cosy place. I was assigned to the same room as the house imam.

I always knew I was gay. So, when the house imam made advances during my second year in college, it did not come as a surprise to me. I did not want it, though. Of course, I strongly resisted; I had left my homosexuality behind with my family and my hometown, and it was part of everything I was running away from—poverty, desperation, isolation, and loneliness. Being gay was now synonymous with my past miserable life. And since I had attached my homosexuality to those feelings, I believe my resistance went beyond internalized homophobia. Homosexuality *was* poverty, desperation, isolation, and loneliness. I wanted none of it. Eventually, though, I gave in. A three-year homosexual relationship began, and I was surprised that no one in the community ever picked up on it. I honestly believe the HM brothers were naïve in that way.

The first time we were together felt wrong. After each interaction, I would boil water to take a shower and burn my body to rid myself of the sinful act. Being together with him and then conducting prayers by standing behind him was dichotomous. Two armies were in constant clash within, and I felt emotionally exhausted. I *was* Blanche in the Streetcar Named Desire; washing off my sins with a hot bath He was also very generous to me. Oftentimes I wondered if I was his mistress because he was providing for me in a secret relationship. These thoughts made it worse, and on one occasion I knowingly hurt myself. My depression was off the roof. During summer breaks, I would leave as early as possible and not come back until it was time to start school. I was trying to have one more night of sleep without him in my bed. I could not tell anyone, and I was not sure my family was actually interested in my mental and physical well-being. I thought that they probably would not want to hear about it. My mother had raised us like there was going to be impending doom any second now. This was the constant atmosphere at home. I was afraid that this might cause that impending doom. At the time, I also had a gay friend, and he would tell me all about his relationship with another guy. Yet, I was unable to talk to him about mine. It was a lonely place that I needed to get out of. That was one reason I decided to go and teach in Uzbekistan after graduation. I wanted to leave my sinful acts behind at the time, and this seemed to be a way out. Oddly enough, I would come back in the summers and see my imam again.

On that note, the accounts about my homosexuality in the preceding paragraph may generate assumptions in the reader's point of view about my inclusion of such intimate detail. I did not provide this account to show another side of the HM. I did not provide this information to give material to opponents of the HM, either. Herein, I provided *my own lived experience* that "names the ordinary and the extraordinary, the quotidian and the exotic, the routine and the surprising, the dull and the ecstatic moments and aspects of experience as we live through them in our human existence" (Van Manen, 2015, p. 39). Hence, this is purely an account of what I lived through in my human experience. It *is* an account of what happened and deserves its place in this book.

The Teacher

My Voyage into HM's Transnational Educational Network

Background

In 1991, the USSR (Union of Soviet Socialist Republics) ceased its existence. There were now new states in Central Asia that no one had ever heard of before. More independence created more need in many ways for these newly free, former USSR states. After the fall, they were no longer behind the iron curtain and many of them shared historical ties with Turkey. The immediate impact of this for Turkey was economic long before it became political and educational. Turkey had a strong textile sector at the time and used that to its advantage to sell goods to the newly independent states. This trade later came to be known as the "suitcase business." People from the newly independent states would buy a cheap plane ticket, come to Istanbul with as many suitcases as they could fit in the plane, buy textile products, put them in those suitcases, and then go back to sell them in shopping centers called *Gum, Sum,* or *Magazines. Gums* and *sums* were large shopping centers while *magazines* were small mom and pop shops owned by locals. In Istanbul, stores put up signs in Russian and hired Russian-speaking sales associates to promote this trade. In the meantime, HM saw the fall of the USSR as an educational opportunity and acted upon it almost immediately. The HM heralds traveled to every Turkic (as well as non-Turkic) state in Central Asia to set up schools and open institutions. This sounds surreal today. One might wonder how someone with no money and language skills would voluntarily just hop on a plane and go somewhere he has never been. There is no answer to that question, but I witnessed it happen. The Central Asian countries the HM heralds went to were Azerbaijan, Bashkortostan, Georgia, Kazakhstan, Kyrgyzstan, Nakhichevan, Tadzhikistan, Turkmenistan, Uzbekistan, and Yakutia. This initiative eventually bore fruit and new schools emerged. The governments, except Uzbekistan, were especially keen on new schools offering quality education in English. The then President Turgut Özal had also actively lobbied for those schools to reestablish the historical ties Turkey had with the region. Teaching at an HM school in Turkey had already become a trend; however, with this new demand, more and more HM college candidates in high schools enrolled in teacher education programs. Those who graduated from college and knew English were almost immediately sent to an HM school in Central Asia. They needed English-speaking teachers for science and math classes there. Usually, there were two sides in a school: The Turkish side provided instruction in biology, chemistry, English, math, physics, computer science, and Turkish; and the local partners provided instruction in history, geography, language and literature, and philosophy. Although from a bilingual education standpoint this would not be ideal practice today, it was a selling point at the time. The schools were all-boys' or all-girls' schools, except elementary schools. The Turkish school personnel consisted of male Muslim and HM administrators and HM teachers—except the girls' schools where the administrators and teachers were mostly Muslim HM females. In time, teacher shortages in those schools grew exponentially and there was an effort to employ some non-HM personnel. However, because of the distance and low wages, this effort was short-lived.

My First Job as a Teacher

After four years in my teacher education program, I was a certified English as a second language teacher. HM elders offered me a position in Central Asia; however, I was indecisive. Initially, I did not want to teach in that locale. Consequently, I was put on hold. I hoped to be appointed to a private HM school in Turkey. I did not want to teach in a Turkish state school because of my previous, horrifying experience in Turkey's educational system.

Eventually, I reconsidered and decided to take the plunge to teach in Central Asia. I wasn't motivated by a compelling reason; however, I was a young and enthusiastic individual, excited to be part of something larger. Preparations were made by Hizmet elders in charge of Central Asia appointments. At the airport, I was redirected to a hangar where planes usually transported goods instead of people. I was surprised. Later, I learned that it was cheaper for the financially broke Uzbek airline to fly out of hangars. I held on to my carry-on bag and stepped onto the plane. I showed my ticket to the flight attendant. She had a blank look pasted on her face. Apparently, there were no seat assignments. Moreover, some seats were occupied by large bags and sacks full of goods. There was one row completely blocked by a man; he was comfortably laying down on his makeshift bed. There was no air-conditioning until the plane took off, either. It was extremely hot inside, and I did not know anyone. This was certainly not one of the flights I took to Europe when I was a child. I started to sweat, and my heart sank.

At landing, the Tashkent airport looked like a scene from a black-and-white Soviet-era movie, and I felt the sharp stench of burnt rubber mixed with airplane gas. I made my way out of the plane and walked to customs. I saw a Russian man in military uniform checking passports. I was certain that the customs officer was a secret KGB agent. Shivers went down my spine as I was handing my passport to him. I was going to be arrested! Thankfully, nothing happened, and we made a safe exit from the airport. I soon realized the rest of the capital city was of the same character. Previously, I thought the things we saw in the movies about the Soviet Union were fictional and did not depict the reality of the places and people who were represented. I was mistaken. As much as movies were exaggerated versions of reality, this place was a tad bit closer to actual life. As we left the airport in a car, I saw that there were three inconspicuous stop signs within 50 yards, and if you did not stop at each, the police gave you a ticket. They were out there to get you. I found that very odd.

Alas, my reality was a movie now. The food was different; the people were unfriendly and overly cautious with their interactions with others. At the risk of arrest, I had to carry a red *Guvahnomah* or foreigner's ID card, issued by the Uzbek state everywhere I went. The Uzbek police harassed my friends several times; on one occasion they tried to arrest a friend on his wedding night due to some residency permit issue he had never heard of before. At first, I was disoriented when I woke up every morning: I thought I was in Istanbul, and it took me some time to get my bearings.

At first, I was going to work at an HM school in a small city called Golestan. Later, I learned that I had been assigned to stay in Tashkent instead. I worked at an all-boys high school where half of the staff was Turkish, and the other half was Uzbek. As was the custom, the Turkish teachers taught biology, chemistry, math, physics, Turkish, and English, while the Uzbek teachers taught social science, citizenship, history, geography, and Uzbek language and literature.

Simply put, my own education from a low-quality teacher-training program at a Turkish state university did not prepare me and I did not know how to teach. On my first day at Tashkent Boys' High School, I was given a book and simply told to go in and teach English to a group of Uzbek students. In college, I did not do any student teaching, never created a lesson plan, and never learned about classroom management. Needless to say, I failed miserably.

I shared my apartment with other three other male HM teachers. The rent was not very expensive, and we lived together for safety reasons. The Uzbek police did random checks and could arrest you on spot for any reason. Having friends around helped prevent one from ending up in a "gulag" with no one hearing back from you again. Living with colleagues also provided a way for me to get used to the country and stay within the HM circle while experiencing culture shock. The downside of this arrangement was we were never short of visitors. Since the apartment was adjacent to the school, whenever there were visitors to the school from Turkey, the Russian school custodian would point at our building. He did not speak any Turkish and our apartment was the only place he could send them. We had many guests.

In time, my disappointment transformed, and I became curious about the people, places, and events unfolding around me: I was witnessing history in the making. The Uzbek people were upset about the corruption, clandestine political machination, and exploitation that was happening in and to their beloved country. The cautiousness and coldness I first experienced as hostility was their coping mechanism. The Uzbeks were trying to survive and adapt to lightning-fast changes occurring in their country as much as they possibly could. When my HM colleagues and I visited families in their homes, the people would do everything to ensure we were comfortable and had a pleasant visit. I remember those moments being my most content and happy at the time.

On one of those visits, my Uzbek hosts shared that in the old days, the Soviet State would assign an informant to spy on other citizens. The state would then assign another informant to spy on the first informant. They also told us stories about creative ways Uzbeks found to work around the system so that they could fulfill their religious and cultural obligations. Some of those stories I found hilarious. For example, almost all Uzbeks are Muslim by faith, and male circumcision is considered a sacred tradition in their culture. However, the Communist Soviet State banned the practice. An Uzbek father wanted his son to be circumcised, so he decided to report himself. When word got to Moscow, the state officials heard there had been a circumcision and chartered a plane for Uzbekistan. They examined the man's son and, seeing the boy was still "intact," the bureaucrats returned to Moscow. Once the team departed, the man had his son circumcised.

Venturing Farther Away from Home and the HM Circle

After three years in Uzbekistan, circa 1997, I asked for reassignment. I did not know what I really wanted to do next at that point. Pursuing a master's degree was an option. When I was assigned to an HM high school in Indonesia, I carried this intention with me. I had never traveled that far from Turkey and was excited to see new places. Before departure, I did not foresee that it was going to be such a long flight. On my arrival, the hot and humid air brushed my face before forcing its way to my lungs and settling there comfortably. Everything looked different and it was as if I had been transported to a different world.

I soon discovered that I was one of the very few teachers from Turkey to ever teach in the school. HM participants in Indonesia were not elder brothers; these "heralds" were young male adults attending college. Admirably, these men had built the first brick-and-mortar HM high school with their hands. However, since the heralds did not yet possess college degrees or teaching credentials, the HM schools in Indonesia replaced them with qualified teachers. I saw that this deficit created great tension; the young HM college students had built a school from scratch, yet they were not honored, but instead gave their school to these new teachers. For example, when high-rank government officials visited the school or there was an event at the Turkish embassy, only HM teachers, not the college students, were asked to go.

Most of the teachers in the schools were single and lived in one house; the unmarried college students lived in another. In all honesty, this arrangement felt like a caste system. Issues between the two groups led to obvious tensions and stressors that I had not witnessed in other HM institutions. Regardless, our 9–12 grade students received the same excellent education as their peers in other HM schools because we all had their best interest at heart.

The first HM school to be established was in the Depok neighborhood of Bogor city, an hour's drive away from Jakarta, the capital city. Eventually, more schools opened in other cities including Semarang, Yogyakarta, and Jakarta. During my time in Indonesia, the country was hit hard by a global economic crisis and the people were financially affected. At the same time, Turkey also suffered a series of earthquakes that claimed thousands of lives. The already tense work environment became worse with such developments and began to wear me down. In hindsight, I now wonder if this eventually pushed me to what HM participants call a "worldly person" who ended up "outside the HM circle."

After spending two years in Indonesia, I moved back to Turkey in 1999. I wanted to discover my options outside the HM. This new world had made me uncomfortable. At first, I took an office job in a hosiery factory, and when that did not work out, I found a teaching position for English as a Second Language (ESL) at a non-HM language teaching center. Outside the HM cocoon for the first time in my adult life, I was forced to survive on my own. This was my purgatory.

I lasted only one year before I returned to the network in 2001 and was hired to teach at a top-rated, private, HM high school in Istanbul. I pondered the reasons for my inability to survive outside the HM. Turkish society was inexplicably divided into ethnic, political, secular, religious, ideological, and cultural factions at an extreme level; it was like another caste system where one had to spend their whole life before they could move up to another class. Once they gave you a label, you carried it for the rest of your life. I also discovered that I had changed and transformed into a person with additional sides to myself and consequently, no longer fit in with HM. I started to question my previously held beliefs. I was now a fully closeted gay individual who had forced himself to live a completely straight life. That did not sit well; I was rowing my boat against the current by denying my true self. However, voicing the questions in my head was over a decade away; though I did not know it, I would eventually earn my doctorate and come out of this tight and messy closet, to finally express my opinions and gender orientation.

The Immigrant

HM Network in the US, and a Disconnection

After two years of teaching ESL at the private HM high school in Istanbul, my life took another turn. In 2003, I became a diversity visa lottery winner, commonly known as the "green card lottery," and prepared to permanently immigrate to the United States. My prayers had been answered; finally, I was going to see the new world and make my dreams come true. While I began inquiring into teaching positions at HM schools in the U.S., my initial efforts at locating a job were futile. The HM network operated differently in the U.S. than in other parts of the world. I had always believed they would not leave me on my own after so many years of service and would easily secure a position at an HM school. I couldn't have been more wrong.

Almost two years after Mr. Gülen came to the U.S. in 1999, the No Child Left Behind (NCLB) Act came into effect. Despite the many shortcomings of this reiteration of the Elementary & Secondary Education Act of 1965, the NCLB Act promoted the implementation of charter schools, in which many HM educators, including former teachers from Uzbekistani schools, found teaching jobs. Because of the HM's focus on STEM, HM teachers who immigrated to the United States were mainly math, chemistry, biology, and physics educators. HM English teachers were not as popular since local educators were fluent, native speakers in the English language arts subject area.

The movement was in transition in the early 2000s and lacked transparency, organization, and altruism in the US. In order to get a job in an HM school in the U.S. at the time, an individual's qualifications were not extremely important. Instead, prospective educators needed to have strong references from prominent elder brothers. Favoritism ran rampant among individuals. Sadly, I was not connected with the higher echelons of the movement and was at a disadvantage. Besides schools, there were many other opportunities to find a job: After Mr. Gülen's arrival to the U.S. in the late 1990s, the HM took root in its new home and flourished with the assistance of an English-language media presence, including the Zaman Daily newspaper, Today's Zaman, and the Fountain magazine. Consequently, interfaith and charity organizations sprouted across the United States, requiring a constant flow of HM participants from Turkey to fulfill personnel needs. However, there was nothing available for me. I was devastated.

Some HM educators also believed that teachers from Turkey were taking away their jobs. One summer I remember volunteering to teach English for a short period of time to teachers from Turkey who had just arrived and were employed to work at charter schools in the Chicagoland area. Most of them had beginning-level English language proficiency and the new school year was only a couple of months away. I asked myself why, if these people were able to secure a teaching position with little to no English, why hadn't there been any positions for me when I had first arrived in the U.S.?

Back in 2003, my interactions to secure a teaching position with HM participants had been a wake-up call. I meditated over it and, sadly, realized that human beings had little seeds in their hearts that were both good and bad, and that with enough fertile ground to flourish, both types of seeds could grow. After witnessing favoritism and experiencing rejection among HM brothers whom I had previously worked with and admired so much in different circumstances, my faith in HM was challenged.

At first, denial set in: I had always lived within the HM circle and had been sure that I was going to be embraced by my brothers in the U.S. as well. The welcome I hoped for did not happen. Then, I thought perhaps those who might be interested in my services did not know I was available. Tragically, the people I was in touch with were simply not interested in my previous commitments and extensive teaching experience.

I stayed in touch with some close friends, but for the most part, I was disconnected from the movement. I felt betrayed and abandoned; I had a family to take care of with no gainful employment and could not afford healthcare. Like many immigrant educators, my years of teaching and advanced degrees seemed to be working against me. To make ends meet for my family, I sold cheap jewelry at a mall in Gurnee, Illinois, for $7 an hour. I became a necklace seller with a master's degree in English Language and Literature. After searching for a job for months, one of the few responses that materialized was a recruiter's phone call from the U.S. military. The other response came from a daycare facility that asked me to change baby diapers. That was a firm no on my part. The link between myself and the HM broke: I joined the U.S. Army.

The U.S. Army was a unique and interesting experience. In Turkey, I had not wanted to serve in the military. I had paid around $10K so that I could serve just twenty-nine days instead of eighteen months. Yet, here I was, trying to get *in* out of desperation. Being new in the country, I thought this experience would be different from the one I'd had with the Turkish military. I was mistaken. However, serving in the U.S. military helped me get acculturated and integrated into American society a great deal. It was part of my transitioning to the dominant culture. Looking back, I have no regrets on this decision.

The Researcher

Life in Graduate School

After serving in the U.S. Army for two years, I returned to graduate school to further my education and marketability as an educator. Three years after my arrival in the United States, in 2006, I was admitted to the doctoral program in the College of Education at the University of Illinois at Urbana-Champaign (UIUC). To this day, I am grateful for the opportunity. What my old homeland was not able to offer, my new country did in abundance.

I was going about my day-to-day life with an initial diagnosis for chronic depression. However, stabilizing my mental and emotional state with medication and therapy took some time. The first couple of years in grad school was a blur. Only after seeking long-term help, did I come to realize and be more aware of my surroundings. During grad school I took classes and, in no particular order, received unemployment, worked as a public-school teacher, office assistant, sales associate, teaching assistant, and language instructor. The Ph.D. journey was long and took me eight years to complete.

My initial research interest was to study Turkish-German bilingual education practices. I was born and raised in Germany and had an immense interest in and longing for the country. However, after my advisor, Dr. Arlette Ingram Willis, learned that HM operated over a hundred charter schools at the time in the U.S., she strongly encouraged me to change my focus. My advisor had been right: HM was the largest and most influential educational initiative imported from the Muslim world during modern times. In this capacity, HM had the potential to impact Western educational systems. After spending almost two decades within the HM movement, I was able to study the topic as a multilingual, transnational, and informed educational researcher. But more importantly, I possessed an LGBTQ+ lens. I shifted my focus. And I am glad that I did; you are reading the result of that monumental shift in my research priorities.

The Research Process during Changing Times

After much excitement, researching the HM at Illinois proved to be very difficult. Having been closely connected to the HM both physically and emotionally was advantageous to the research process: I had lived, experienced, and observed life as an insider to the community. This proximity also proved to be disadvantageous because I had been financially dependent on the HM while working in their schools. Simply put, I had not known any other way. I lived like HM; thought like HM; and practiced and preached like HM. Looking back, such an intimate stance might have narrowed my focus.

However, after immigrating to the U.S., circumstances had pushed me outside HM; without any vacancies, I'd had to find a job elsewhere. In HM's terms, I was now living "outside the circle". By the time I reached the dissertation stage of my doctoral studies around 2009, there were already mountains between myself and HM. As a result, conducting my research ended up taking a long time. During my graduate work, gaining access to the network, especially Mr. Gülen's close circle, took great effort as I tried hard to reconnect with HM participants. Fortunately, an HM intercultural organization had been founded at UIUC. The group organized summer trips to Turkey for non-HM academics: in other words, Western scholars. In the summer of 2008, I was asked to serve as their guide on the trip. Upon our arrival to Istanbul, we were greeted by an oversized banner hanging over a bridge on a busy highway, advertising an HM-sponsored Turkish Olympiad. I was honestly shocked! I was used to seeing HM as a closer knit, small group of people away from public attention. Apparently, times had changed. Because the ruling (Justice Development Party (JDP) and HM were engaged in a symbiotic relationship at the time, being an HM member was an "in" thing or popular association. During this period, some elder brothers from HM became parliamentary members of the JDP. HM was as famous as a pop star. We did not know at the time, but it was destined to become a one-hit wonder in Turkey.

After my return to Champaign-Urbana, my work on the dissertation began in earnest. My research focused on bilingual education practices and home language support in HM-related schools in the US. Members from the same HM intercultural organization had served as a community of volunteers that created the largest chain of charter schools in the U.S. In order to meet staffing demands, HM imported a steady flow of teachers from Turkey with credentials in science, technology, engineering, and math (STEM). District report cards from the HM charter schools demonstrated that their programs met academic benchmarks in their respective states. Conducting research on those charter schools was important because their students came from underserved communities with a home language other than English. I initially wanted to learn what they were doing in terms of bilingual education that may have contributed to this success.

The process was arduous. First, I had to get in touch with an elder in Chicago and prepare a presentation for him, in order to get access to resources, especially Mr. Fethullah Gülen. Although it was not difficult to convince the elder in Chicago on why there was a need for research on the HM and its operations in the U.S. education sector, it was extremely difficult to gain access to Mr. Gülen. At the time, he lived in Pennsylvania, and taking a trip there with my student budget, waiting in his living compound for days just to see him for a short time, and then asking for an interview, were both financially and emotionally draining. Some other movement participants were also reluctant to grant an interview. I was in school, worked full-time, and was trying to provide for my children. I switched many jobs and took every opportunity that came my way so I could stay financially afloat. There were times when I seriously considered leaving everything behind and flipping burgers for a living in sunny Florida! In the end, I finished my research, defended my dissertation, and got my first academic job. What you are reading here is the result of that long journey, which I will be glad to never take again.

· 2 ·

THE HISTORY

Historical Overview of the Hizmet Movement and Mr. Gülen's Life

The Hizmet Movement (HM) is a social movement that started in the late 1960s. Graham Fuller (2014), a former operations officer in the U.S. Central Intelligence Agency (CIA) and former vice-chairman of the National Intelligence Council (NIC), describes the HM as "a unique grassroots organization" that has emerged on the global scene, characterized by unique philosophical and social traits. Fuller (2014) notes that HM participants profess their faith through volunteerism; have a goal to serve all humanity; embrace both science and faith as "complementary concepts"; promote religious and ethnic tolerance; and defer from "confrontation with the West"; while engaging in communal dialogue (p. 154). Fuller's definition of HM is not the only one. Today, there are many publications that define, argue, describe what HM is or is not. One of the more recent descriptions is by Paul Weller (2022). According to Weller, HM can be characterized as

> a network of congregants, recordings, books, sohbets (or, meetings) that has developed in interactive engagement with the emergence of Fethullah Gülen as a figure who has religiously inspired, intellectually articulated and practically initiated a distinctive

action- and reflection-oriented hermeneutic of Anatolian and Sufi-inflected Sunni Islam into a dynamic and organic set of networked initiatives including dormitories (often known as "lighthouses"), schools, businesses, media enterprises, business and other initiatives that have a relationship with one another in terms of mutual engagement, learning and challenge. (Weller, 2022, p. 28)

What follows is a brief history of the Turkish Republic, and HM intertwined with Mr. Fethullah Gülen's life.

Early Roots of HM and the New Turkish Republic

The HM's formative and deepest roots coincide with the birth of the Turkish Republic in 1923. Initially known as the Nur or "Divine Light" Movement, the HM was founded under the leadership of Bediüzzaman Said Nursi, an advocate of Islamic reform. He was a charismatic Kurdish-Turkish Islamic visionary whose philosophy did not overlap with the new secular Turkish state. Therefore, he was arrested, poisoned, tortured, and exiled numerous times during his life. Nursi wanted a "religious revival taking place, not through the medium of political activism or violent revolution, but rather through a principle that he defined as 'positive action' (*müspet hareket*)" (Tee, 2021, p. 89). He was the person Gülen received his inspiration from. Nursi started to write the *Risale-i Nur*, or Epistles of Light, around 1925. This was a collection of six books: *Sözler* or the Words, *Mektûbat* or the Letters, *Lem'alar* or the Flashes, *Şuâlar* or the Rays, *İşârât-ül I'caz* or the Signs of Miraculousness, and the *Asa-yı Musa* or the Staff of Moses. These books were concerned with interpreting Qur'an basically in a way that raises the faithful and intellectual level among people. Through his messages, he was able to resist atheism, unbelief, and the heresies that Turkey spread to create a generation who does not believe in Allah or his prophet" (Samarh, 2021, p. 909). Nursi's work deeply impacted Gülen and "shaped Gülen's effort to unite "mind" and "heart" in learning as an advocate for civil Islam..." (Pahl, 2019, p. 58).

In 1923, the establishment of the new Turkish Republic by Mustafa Kemal Atatürk turned the country's back to a 600-year-old Ottoman history, drawing a sharp line between the past and the present. The Ottoman Empire had previously set up a governing system based on Islamic values that welcomed non-Muslims as well. However, while acknowledging its past from a nationalist point of view, the new state denied any past political and religious association with its predecessor and Islamic values because "a primary goal of Turkey's Kemalist regime was to suppress Anatolia's Ottoman-Islamic tradition by taking over the definition and application of faith, education, and law in Turkish society" (Hendrick, 2013, p. 16). The new Turkish Republic pioneered a completely Western way of life that the system saw to be the only way for advancement.

Toward this end, the Turkish parliament abolished the title and role of the sultanate and the caliphate, similar to the Catholic Pope. The new government then carried out a number of other actions: They eliminated the Islamic law or sharia and madrasa schools for Islamic instruction. The authorities shut down Dervish monastery houses permanently as well. Moreover, they banned Kurdish publications and the veil, an important religious attire as well as the fez, which had historically served as a symbol of the Ottoman government.

The extensive reforms additionally replaced the Ottoman alphabet, written in Arabic letters with Latin script. After changing the written code, religious practices were strongly encouraged to be conducted in Turkish (Çetin, 2010, pp. 12–17). An era of laicism began, a period defined by the founder of the republic as "not a mere separation between religion and worldly affairs. It is the freedom of conscience, religion, and worship" (Atatürk, 2014).

Against the backdrop of these dramatic changes, the last emperor, Sultan Vahdettin, left Istanbul for good on March 17, 1922 on British warship Malaya. By March 15, 1924, there was no one left in Turkey from the Ottoman Dynasty (Hasanoglu, 2012). A completely sterilized, secular system was implemented, favoring only Atatürk's philosophical and political principles; those people who did not conform to such beliefs or behaviors received harsh treatment.

In the middle of such extreme revisions, a new class of ruling elite rose to power. This new class, coined as Homo LASTus (Laicist, Atatürkist, Sunni Muslim, Turkish) by Yılmaz (2015, pp. 9–10), adopted Western values; supported Atatürk's ideas unconditionally; and welcomed all changes that came down from him regardless of their previous affiliations. In return, they acquired new power and privileges exclusive to them. The new ruling elite had access to state property; were placed in important positions in the government; and received tremendous financial support in the form of tax breaks, use of government resources, and other state enterprises.

The 1940s and 1950s: The Ontogenesis of a Leader

From 1923 until the 1950s, Turkey was governed under a one-party dictatorship (Tüfekyapan, 2017). The eventual transition to a multi-party democracy brought the Democrat Party (DP) into power in 1950. However, as Tachau (2000) noted, "despite the DP's victory, the old centrist elite was not totally bereft of influence", eventually leading to a military coup in 1960 (p. 131).

The Era of the Democrat Party

During its ten-year rule, the DP created new socioeconomic classes and "an upward social mobility became a widespread phenomenon" (Tachau, 2000, p. 132) under the leadership of Adnan Menderes. The political party also doubled its budget on education compared to previous years and opened new universities (Karakök, 2011, p. 97). The public grew an optimistic outlook for the future as a result of the positive economic, educational, and social developments. In addition, the DP gained more approval when it legalized the Arabic call to prayer, which had been previously elicited in Turkish. However, this change in language proved unsettling for members of the military.

Toward the end of the 1950s, the optimism and developments cultivated in society were clouded when the "DP began treating the opposition as illegitimate, and, after the 1957 election, manifested the perspective and behavior of an authoritarian party" (Tachau, 2000, p. 133). The manner in which the DP governed the country in the late 1950s eventually led to a coup on May 27, 1960. The military overthrew the government and executed Prime Minister Adnan Menderes at the gallows.

Gülen Comes of Age

During this time, the founder of the Hizmet Movement (HM), Fethullah Gülen, was born in 1941 in a small village of Erzurum, Turkey (Çetin, 2010, p. 20). Gülen's father was an imam, and his mother was a homemaker. The boy was the second child in a family that would consist of eight children. Although almost all religious instruction and practice was officially forbidden during his childhood, Gülen read the entire Quran when he was only five years old and completely memorized the holy text at ten.

The child received an education styled on the Islamic madrasas that had been banned in the modern Turkish Republic. Instead, the former madrasa teachers taught the boy secretly in their private homes. These Islamic scholars, highly respected in their communities and areas of expertise, included Gülen's own father, Ramiz Bey, the Nakşibendi Sheikh Muhammed Lütfi Efendi, Rasim Baba, Osman Bektaş, Solakzade Sadık Efendi, and Sıddık Efendi (Yavuz, 2013, pp. 29–30). The young boy was engaged in *sohbets*, or small-group talks of religious nature, conducted by prominent Sufi masters, as a part of the curriculum.

Apart from Gülen's religious education, the young Gülen was also obligated to attend a public elementary school. However, a lapse in the boy's early education occurred when his father was assigned to a mosque in Alvar Köyü, a village near Erzurum after the family moved. Their new home was located in a small village that did not have any schools at the time. In the late 1950's, Gülen acquired his high school diploma through an adult education program when two important events occurred in his life. Çetin (2010) states the young man "came across compilations of the scholarly work Risale-i Nur (Epistles of Light) by Said Nursi…, [and] sat for and passed the state exam to become an imam and preacher" (p. 24). As the result of high scores, Gülen was assigned by the state to a prestigious landmark mosque as an assistant imam in city of Edirne. The second event, the Epistles of Light, later became an indispensable component of required readings in the Light Houses—or homes where HM college students would reside.

The 1960s: Turkey Faces Its First Military Coup

After the first coup d'état of the new Turkish Republic on May 27, 1960, Turkey witnessed three more rebellions in 1971, 1980, and 1997 respectively. These rebellions "largely came in times of crisis when civil-military relations were strained… and the army command perceived that the country was in mortal danger due to anti-state activities that the state could not control" (Narlı, 2000, p. 117).

According to Daldal (2004), the 1960 coup d'état was the work of a new, privileged, middle class comprised of a variety of professionals including educators, military personnel, media members, and other stakeholders. This advantaged faction of society not only wanted to eliminate the DP government, but also sought "to pursue the Jacobin–Kemalist tradition [of modernizing reforms] in opposition to the liberal–conservative outlook; a continuation of an intra-elite conflict that dated back to the pre-republican period" (p. 76).

Gülen in an Era of Political Turmoil

During this period, Gülen began his mandatory military service required by all Turkish males in the capital city of Ankara. He was later transferred to the city of İskenderun where "his commanding officer assigned to him the duty of lecturing soldiers on faith and morality, and, recognizing Gülen's intellectual ability, gave him many Western classics to read" (Çetin, 2010, pp. 30–31). These texts opened a fresh, new window to him, introducing the young man to a new way of life that exposed him to schools of thought different than he had previously known. Perhaps most importantly, Gülen became more informed on democracy. Much later in his life, in 1994 at the Journalists and Writers Foundation, the scholar would emphasize that Turkey needed democracy, and that only 10% of Turkish society had previously been exposed to democratic values and practices up to that point in time. During his prolific speech at the commencement reception, Gülen would conclude that "from now on, both in Turkey and in the rest of the world, there will be no going back from democracy" (GulenMovement, 2012).

Aslandoğan (2014) describes such support in the early 1990s as being significant, in light of the fact that conservative Muslims in Turkey had "mixed" emotions toward democracy. Indeed, many Islamic scholars/Muslims espoused the idea that democracy and Islam were contradictory or in conflict with each other. However, "Gülen argued that there are no essential incompatibilities, and it is in fact the best, the most compatible form of governance with Islamic principles that pertained to governance" (AfSV_USA, 2014).

HM Is Born

In the early 1960s, the small group of pioneers became more invested in Turkey's youth. Concerned by the number of children and teenagers "being attracted into extremist, radical ideologies, including atheistic communism and materialism," Gülen took the initiative to promote and instill universal moral values (Ebaugh, 2010, p. 28). As a part of this initiative in 1963, Ebaugh (2010) described Gülen leading "the Turkish Association for Struggle Against Communism in Erzurum and later on recruited ideological support against the political threat of Iranian Islam" (p. 26). In 1964, the Turkish state, under the secular 28th Government, reassigned Gülen from Edirne and to Kırklareli in 1965 where he would work as a preacher for the one year.

A year later in 1966, Gülen was assigned an appointment in the city of İzmir. As the head preacher, Gülen "held managerial responsibility for a mosque, a student study and boarding-hall, and for preaching in the Aegean region" (Çetin, 2010, p. 31). Those activities were later extended to summer camps.

This five-year period in İzmir would be described as Kestanepazarı days by HM participants later in HM circles, which referred to the part of the city where Gülen had worked and lived. During this time, the imam did not get paid—nor did he wish remuneration—for his services and "remained distanced from the financial management of all institutions related to the movement. Instead, he encouraged the sponsors of these institutions to actively oversee the use of their monies. These actions cultivated "great trust in Gülen's honesty and integrity" (Ebaugh, 2010, p. 37). Abdullah Aymaz (2014), a life-long friend of Gülen who managed the library in İzmir, highlights that the actual HM started to form after Gülen's arrival in Kestanepazarı, a small part of the İzmir city. Hence, the 1960s serve as a turning point for the birth, formulation, and initial momentum of the movement. The ideological community, while pleasing to some, displeased many others as an unofficial religious/social community.

Concerns, Curriculum, and Community of Kestanepazarı Days

Under Gülen's direction, the student dormitories housing male youth between ages 11–18 were followed by summer camps, also known as the *Kamp*. Because summer breaks can last as long as three months in Turkey, the circle of followers were concerned students would be exposed to harmful influences while away from their regular studies and life in the dorms. Summer camps fulfilled the mission to fight off negative effects and further unify the community. These camps served as spiritual retreats.

The first camps were held outside the city of İzmir, away from the watchful eyes of the Kemalist state. The location for these summer camps was near a river or a stream so that the students and their teachers would have potable water. The group would sleep in tents and use a temporary latrine made of bricks. For these summer camps, Gülen put together a one-month long informal, yet very rigorous curriculum. The youth spent most of the day reading the *Risale-i Nur Külliyatı* or Epistles of Light collection. The main volumes in the collection consisted of six books. Those who were new participants would start with *Sözler* or Words because it was an easier read. Then the students would usually move on to other books in the collection and read *Mektûbat* or the Letters, *Lem'alar* or the Flashes, *Şuâlar* or the Rays, *İşârât-ül I'caz* or the Signs of Miraculousness, and the *Asa-yı Musa* or the Staff of Moses. They would finish reading the whole collection while in camp. They also prayed namaz or Islamic prayers five times a day, did *tesbihat* or invocations after each namaz prayer, participated in *sohbets* or small-group talks of religious nature and *ilmihal* or Islamic catechism lessons, read religious stories, and learned *fıkıh* or Islamic jurisprudence. Participants prayed together, read the Quran and the Epistles of Light, learned more about Islam, and strengthened their brotherhood with other youth of their age.

These summer camps could be fun as well: For example, the students would call each other *şakirt* or student. This is a non-Turkish word and newcomers to the HM would not know the meaning. Through the night, students would take turns keeping watch for safety. People would come in and ask the next *şakirt* to wake up and keep watch. This bothered one of those newcomers as it kept waking him up each time. He eventually got up in frustration and yelled, "Hey şakirt dude, whoever you are just get up and go keep watch!" This resulted in a lot of laughter.

Over the years as the movement grew, these summer camps or spiritual retreats transformed and moved indoors, evolving into "house camps", "dorm camps", and eventually "hotel camps" in the U.S. Because most of the HM participants were young, single young adults or couples just starting families, camp organizers were easily able to accommodate participants twice a year in dorms or student apartments without logistical issues. These newer camps were initially subsidized with monies from HM businesspeople as well. Today, HM devotees in the U.S. maintain tradition once a year during the winter break for seven to ten days convening in "hotel camps" at their own expense with families and friends.

Regardless, the concerns, curriculum, and community that established dorms and summer camps eventually led the way to the establishment of a network of HM private schools.

The 1970s: Another Rebellion and Gülen's Arrest

The next decade of Turkish politics was as rough and difficult as the previous era. There were street demonstrations and Marxist movements had started to take hold. There were also bombings, robberies, and kidnappings. Universities became dysfunctional and college students engaged in urban guerrilla warfare. At that point, the Military Memorandum of March 12, 1971, made a significant mark on the country's political history. The purpose of the memorandum was to put an end to the civil unrest and help establish a strong government rooted in Atatürk's principles. Nihat Erim, the 13th prime minister of the Republic of Turkey for nearly fourteen months from March 1971 to May 1972, called the memorandum "the result of more than a century's yearning and striving for democracy" (Erim, 1972, p. 246). After the memorandum was announced, the military seized power and the elected government dissolved.

Erim (1972) justified the intervention of the military by stating, "It is only natural that when the Republic and the country is in danger the armed forces step in to defend them" (p. 248). He asserted student protests had turned into armed conflicts between the far-right, who represented the ultranationalists, and radical left, comprised of the labor unions, resulted from training and provocation by unnamed forces outside Turkey. In alliance with the Kemalist left, Erim painted the picture very grimly, arguing that foreign, professionally-trained, and heavily fortified combatants had infiltrated the motherland and recruited leftist students for guerrilla warfare. He portrayed that people were hijacked and killed; bombings shattered windows, setting cars ablaze. Erim further (1972) claimed that on one hand, communist terrorists had taken universities hostage and were using public and state institutions of higher learning to stock weapons in an armed effort to transform Turkey into a communist republic. On the other, the right prepared counter attacks at a level of violence leading to civil war. Erim's portrayal of the conflict served as a rationale for state interference, declaring that:

> it was at this point that the High Command of the Armed Forces reluctantly intervened [because] the social and economic structure of the country was in need of fundamental changes. With a population growing more than a million per year and the economic gap between regions being very deep, the situation created a fertile ground for extremism. (Erim, 1972, p. 249)

The military eventually intervened by way of coup by memorandum; the prime minister Süleyman Demirel resigned; and social order was restored for almost another decade until another coup on September 12, 1980.

HM's Expansion and Issues with Authorities

After the Memorandum of March 12 in 1971, Gülen was arrested and jailed for six months. The authorities later let him go without charges. When he pressed the police to provide a reason for his detention, they explained that since so many leftists had been detained, the authorities had "needed to arrest some prominent Muslims in order to avoid being accused of unfairness" (Çetin, 2010, p. 31). Upon his release, government officials did not allow Gülen to preach for a very brief period.

In 1972, he was reassigned by the Turkish Directorate of Religious Affairs from his post in İzmir to serve as an imam in Edremit. A subsequent reassignment to Manisa followed in 1974, followed by a transfer back to Bornova district in İzmir in 1976. The reasons for his frequent reassignments remain unknown; however, this is not unusual in Turkey.

Upon his return to İzmir in the mid-70s, the work to establish dorms and residence halls for middle and high school students started in earnest. These efforts took off and snowballed into the 1980s, reaching youth in attendance at colleges and universities. Adolescents and young adults had become extremely polarized from the rest of society, impacted by communist and ultra-nationalist ideas, especially in higher education. Ebaugh (2010) explains parents characterized HM dorms and residence halls as sanctuaries for their children, because alcohol and drug use, sexual misconduct, and ideological indoctrination were prohibited. Hence, "many conservative and religious parents encouraged their children to live in the dormitories as they attended university in the big cities in Turkey" (Ebaugh, 2010, p. 28).

A Humble Beginning for HM College Preparation Courses

In the 1970s, the HM ventured into a new initiative and started helping students with their college preparation exams. This was received with great enthusiasm because the Turkish public school system was all but defunct and could not provide enough support for students to pass extremely difficult centralized college entrance examinations.

During this time of growth in the mid-1970s, Gülen "managed to establish lighthouses and created a web of networks to realize his dream of cultivating a new generation of religious revivalists" (Yavuz, 2013, p. 36). By 1977, the imam was "one of the three most widely recognized and influential preachers in Turkey," prompting visits from the prime minister and other state officials at his Friday sermons (Çetin, 2010, p. 37). Across the 1970s–1990s, these popular sermons largely focused on topics related to the exemplary lives of the Prophet Mohammad and his disciples. The sermons used a storytelling method to address moral and ethical issues in Islam. Gülen's unique oral storytelling skills scaffolded what was otherwise complex content for audiences, making the information and mode of communication accessible. Indeed, Yavuz (2013) describes Gülen as "the best religious storyteller in Turkey" (p. 112).

At the end of the decade, the HM's monthly, Sufi-oriented periodical called *Sızıntı* began publication in 1979 ("Fethullah Gülen's life," 2002). Today, the periodical is published in English only, under the name of the Fountain. From the establishment of youth housing to college preparation curriculum, the publication of the *Sızıntı* affirmed the pedagogy and principles of the HM had expanded as a sociocultural movement from private to public spheres.

The 1980s: From a Communal to an Institutional Entity

In the midst of these accomplishments, Gulen and his followers were well aware of increasing political unrest. On September 12, 1980, Turkey witnessed its third military coup within twenty years. Similar to other times of crisis, when the privileged, secular, ruling class thought the government and Atatürkist/Kemalist way of life were under threat, the military intervened. As Narlı (2000) explains, the Turkish military was considered to be the guardian of the republic and Atatürk's six principles comprised of Secularism, Republicanism, Populism, Statism, Revolutionism, and Nationalism (p. 108).

However, the military was also a staunch proponent of Westernization and saw Islamic—Islamist in Narlı's terms—movements as a barrier to westernization, democracy, and Atatürk's ideal to elevate the Turkish Republic to the level of contemporary/modern civilizations. Headed under the command of chief of staff General Kenan Evren, the military "intervened politically to counter forces blocking this transformation and to preserve democracy, secularism, and national unity in the face of Islamist, separatist, and sectarian challenges" (Narlı, 2000, p. 108). Hence, General Kenan Evren announced the armed forces had no choice but to seize control of the government. Evren claimed that the armed forces wanted to (1) provide the happiness and prosperity the glorious Turkish nation deserved; (2) secure the nation's unity; (3) strengthen and operationalize Atatürk's/Kemalism's six principles that individuals and groups had deliberately tried to weaken; (4) re-stabilize the democratic society back onto solid foundations; and (5) re-establish the withered state authority (Evren, 1980, p. 5).

The HM as an Institutional Entity

In light of these political developments, Islamic scholars like Gülen had no choice but to hide to secure their safety, initiatives, and lives when the coup took place. Regardless, Gülen was briefly arrested and then let go after six hours. Six months after the September 12, 1980, military coup, citing undisclosed health conditions, Gülen stopped preaching and resigned from his imam position in 1981.

In the meantime, the military government actively created and imposed a new Kemalist Muslimism on conservative Turkish citizens, believing their "new" Muslim prototype would not conflict with the secular, Kemalist state or foster a sense of exclusion (Yılmaz, 2015, p. 67). Yılmaz (2015) asserts these actions led to the creation of a pious image of Atatürk himself. Later, when this mirage was rendered insufficient, General Evren would insert his own eclectic opinions on religion as the "real Islam" (p. 67).

Consequently, religious instruction became mandatory in public schools and the number of imam-hatip schools (state schools training Muslim preachers) increased. Additionally, the Directorate of Religious Affairs became a constitutional entity and the Islamic Süleyman Efendi community operated courses to teach the Quran (Yılmaz, 2015, p. 67). These actions were not executed in the name of freedom of religion; rather, the initiatives were the part of the Turkish military's plan to multiply the number of Kemalist Muslims. However, within two decades, their plan proved to be counter-productive when the power structure would give rise to conservative political Islam.

The 1980s also became known as the Özal decade. Turgut Özal was the 26th prime minister and 8th president of Turkey. The statesman adopted a liberal, free-market approach to the economy and established closer ties with the European countries e.g., Germany, France, Britain, and Italy. During his tenure in office, the economy, albeit slowly, picked up pace and the private sector became more visible. Moreover, the prime minister made it his mission to go beyond the country's borders and reach out to Turks in the Balkans and newly, independent Central Asian countries after the fall of the Soviet Union. In the 1990s, Özal would go on to actively advocate for newly opened HM schools in those countries. A religious person himself, Özal observed the Muslim pilgrimage of Hajj, an event that seriously disturbed Kemalists and the military at the time.

Meanwhile, the Turkish state issued yet another order for Gülen's arrest while in Medina on his third pilgrimage due to claims regarding his involvement with the Mehmet Özyurt criminal case. Mehmet Özyurt was from Hatay city and was a close friend of Mr. Gülen. They also resembled each other, so much so that when Mr. Gülen was away from the mosque, Mehmet Özyurt would take the stand and no one could tell the difference. Özyurt was arrested on the grounds that he wanted to dismantle the constitutional order of the Turkish Republic. This was based on false testimony (Özer, 2008, p. 157). He was later acquitted. In time, the imam only preached on Fridays in various mosques, mainly around İstanbul and İzmir. These sermons were later published in a three-volume series entitled, The Infinite Light.

All in all, the decade wasn't filled with all bad news for HM: in 1982, Yamanlar College—HM's first private high school—opened in Izmir. Additionally, the movement's first newspaper, the Zaman Daily, went into print in 1986. The English version of the periodical, Today's Zaman, followed some twenty-one years later. In summary, during the 1980s, the HM ceased to operate like a small community; while still preserving that tight-knit spirit, the movement morphed into an institutional entity.

1990s: More Complications for Turkish Democracy

During the 1990s, another conservative, openly Islamist party, called the Welfare Party (WP), came into power. The WP formed a coalition with the center-right True Path Party after the 1996 elections. This newly formed government coalition sounded the alarm bells for Kemalist elites of the deep state because Necmettin Erbakan, the WP's leader and new prime minister, did not value nor emphasize relationships with the West in the same manner as his predecessor. Erbakan had different ideas in stark contrast to the secular state; he wanted to establish an Islamic coalition similar to the North Atlantic Treaty Organization (NATO). Erbakan named this Islamic coalition an Islamic Economic Union.

The WP also expressed anti-Kemalist views until the Turkish military finally "lost patience.... and sent [Erbakan] a memorandum ordering him to step down" (Fuller, 2014, pp. 71). This action came to be known as Turkey's post-modern coup. Erbakan resigned and the Supreme Court closed the WP in 1998.

However, three years later in 2001, Erbakan's WP gave birth to the JDP, led by Recep Tayyip Erdoğan. As of 2023, the JDP has been in power for the last twenty-two years. Initially, the JDP was perceived as "a conservative, democratic mass party that situates itself at the center of the political spectrum," and as a "reformist," "realistic," "pro-change," and "principled" party (Gündem, 2005, p. xxxii). This positive view, however, would change during the JDP's second term.

The 1998 post-modern coup, like its predecessors, was the result of multiple decades of ideological warfare that embroiled Turkish politics. This political conflict not only caused coups but created and consolidated two distinct bodies in the system including the permanent, Kemalist state and a temporary, disposable government. The former consisted of the Kemalist/Atatürkist ruling elite who exercised tremendous power over the military, judiciary, and media for many generations. The permanent, Kemalist state was the guard of Atatürk's principles, culture, and secular way of life the "Father of the Turks" had pioneered.

Governments, however, were impermanent entities existing in the present at the disposal of the state. Up to this point in Turkish politics, governments could come and go, or—if necessary—be overthrown. The JDP would later change the transitory nature of governance during its third term by coalescing the state and the government into one oppressive entity in the new millennium.

The HM Goes Global

The role of the media in Turkish society would extend its reach when the first private TV channel, Star 1 TV, was launched in the 1990s. A flood of other media organizations soon followed suit. Voices from outside the Kemalist perspective became widely accessible, extensively appealing to a variety of demographic groups and sub-cultures for the first time in Turkey. This new free and open market economy took the Kemalists by surprise as their ideological base expanded from "subjects such as Islam and Islamism...[to]...theses that they had never heard about before" communicated on television screens in their own private living rooms (Yılmaz, 2015, p. 68).

Among the available programs, in 1993, the Samanyolu Broadcasting Group, SBG, aired HM's first TV channel called Samanyolu TV. Their broadcasts quickly expanded to countries in West and Central Asia, including Azerbaijan, Armenia, Georgia, Nakhichevan, and Turkmenistan in 1996. As the popularity of the HM's message grew, the SBG began to broadcast in Europe and North Africa in 1999; a global consciousness of the HM principles developed in countries such as Egypt, Iraq, Germany, the United Kingdom, and Austria. Samanyolu TV eventually aired in North America in 2000 and reached Canadian and U.S. audiences, albeit for a short time. At the time, the SBG grew exponentially to include 8 TV channels—Mehtap TV, Samanyolu Haber TV, Ebru TV, Yumurcak TV, Samanyolu Avrupa TV, Samanyolu US, and Samanyolu TV before ceasing operation in 2016 as a result of harassment from the JDP government ("Samanyolu TV," 2017).

In 1991, Gülen stopped offering sermons in mosques because "he felt that some people were trying to manipulate or exploit his presence and the presence of the Movement participants at [the] large public gatherings" (Çetin, 2012, p. 20). Instead, the imam began to conduct sohbets, or small-group talks, covering a wide arrange of topics such as spirituality, religion, and current issues, currently available at herkul.org.

In a parallel development, HM's educational initiatives snowballed, branching out from Nakhichevan in West Asia to Kazakhstan in Central Asia. This initiative transformed and solidified HM into a global phenomenon. In the beginning, after the fall of the Soviet Union in 1992, the HM founded a school in Nakhichevan City in Nakhichevan by Azerbaijani President Haydar Aliyev; his Secretary of Education Nazım Ekberov; and İlhan İşbilen, the CEO of Zaman Daily Newspaper (Özcan, 2012). This noteworthy school was the first HM institution to be established outside of Turkey.

After establishing Nakhichevan, Gülen and his followers opened hundreds of other schools in other West and Central Asian nations including Bashkortostan, Afghanistan, Georgia, Kazakhstan, Kyrgyzstan, Uzbekistan, Tajikistan, and Turkmenistan, among other countries. Students in these HM schools were held to high academic standards and received instruction in the English language. Many also learned Turkish as an additional language. HM school students often graduated as trilingual speakers, attending prestigious colleges such as Bosphorus University in Turkey, Oxford University in the United Kingdom, and Harvard University in the United States. In time, additional HM schools, interfaith dialogue organizations, and charity initiatives were founded in other countries, as far as Indonesia, Singapore, Madagascar, China, South Africa, and Australia.

In 1994, HM intellectuals established their own scholarly organization called the Journalists and Writers Foundation (JWF) on the Anatolian side of Istanbul with Gülen serving as the honorary president of the foundation since its inception. The JWF's primary goal was to fight poverty, ignorance, and inter-faith and inter-cultural conflict in Turkey. The foundation later pioneered the Abant Platform, an annual forum that sought "to strengthen democracy by fostering dialogue on important issues and by believing that all different groups should be able to express themselves freely" (Journalists and Writers Foundation, 1998). The participants at the Abant Platform included politicians, academics, journalists, and other prominent figures from all walks of life in Turkey.

In 1996, the network's first institution of higher education, Fatih University, opened its doors in Istanbul. As of November 2010, six years before Erdoğan's JDP government closed the school, it enrolled 1,703 students in associate degree programs; 8,157 students in undergraduate or baccalaureate programs; and 1,460 students in postgraduate programs (Fatih Üniversitesi, 2010).

HM Goes For-Profit

During this time, the HM found additional ways to fund its activities in Turkey. HM opened its first, interest-free bank, Bank Asya, the same year in 1996. Other HM businesses followed in Turkey. The majority of these small enterprises were affiliated with Kaynak Holding, an umbrella company, which headquartered 23 different HM businesses. For example, Işık Yayınları sold spiritual books, while Sürat Teknoloji provided internet and technology (IT) services and solutions to institutions. In the K-12 education sector, Gökkuşağı Publications sold schoolbooks, supplies, and toys. Kaynak Kağıt manufactured paper and Çağlayan provided large scale printing services in addition to selling Xerox/printing machines. The HM also entered the food and travel industry: İtina sold dairy, poultry and meat products to businesses across Turkey; Nüanstur offered hotel reservations, domestic and international leisure travel, and Hajj and Umre services for traveler who wanted to go on religious and culture tours. Last, but not least, Sürat Kargo, a delivery services company like Fedex, offered all kinds of freight shipment services from small packages to large shipments for individuals, businesses, and agencies (The Global Entrepreneurship Network, 2021). This explosion of business activity was significant to HM because it provided secure employment for HM participants, capital for future initiatives, and received public attention—albeit not always positive.

Interfaith Dialogue and the U.S. Chapter

Such educational and economical advances further elevated the status of the HM community, positioning its followers a seat on the global stage of interfaith dialogue. In 1996, Gülen met with Turkey's chief rabbi, David Aseo, and Bartholomew I, the Patriarch of the Fener Roman Orthodox Church in Istanbul. In 1998, he journeyed to Italy for an audience with Pope John Paul II in the Vatican. Despite the ancient history of Islam, these events were highly significant because Gülen was the first Muslim Turkish scholar to engage in such talks. The imam's discussions with the head of the Roman Catholic Church, a religion represented by less than 1% of Turks (Pew Research Center, 2016), demonstrated that the HM's interfaith dialogue transcended beyond the movement's homeland of Turkey.

True to his character, Gülen did not stop at meetings with international religious leaders. In the name of interfaith dialogue in Turkey, he expressed his public support to reopen the Theological School of Halki, formerly run by the Eastern Orthodox Church. The institution closed its doors on its own in 1971 after the Nihat Erim government mandated that all higher education institutions in Turkey, regardless of affiliation, be under the governance of the Turkish state. (Gündem, 2005, pp. 44–45). During the mid to late 1990s, Gülen also advocated for and supported Turkey's European Union membership, a group with 27 countries in Europe that "enables most goods, services, money and people to move freely" (European Commission, 2020, p. 7). He saw this as an opportunity to encourage the country's democratization process.

In 1999, Gülen eventually came to the United States to receive medical treatment for cardiac dysrhythmia, diabetics, and heart problems. At the turn of the decade, HM's headquarters informally moved to the Pocono Mountains in the state of Pennsylvania where Gülen was residing. This shift in location drove other—and younger—HM participants to the U.S. as well. As a movement rooted in the educational process, the timing perfectly coincided with as charter schools in the United States expanded. Consequently, many first and second-generation HM participants were employed as teachers and other school personnel positions in U.S. charter schools founded and operated by HM in Illinois, Texas, Ohio, California, to name a few.

The 2000s: HM's Ups and Downs

The new millennium witnessed tremors caused by power shifts in Turkish politics. As the mayor of Istanbul, Recep Tayyip Erdoğan was arrested, jailed, and banned from politics for life for referencing a poem written in 1912 by Turkish poet Ziya Gökalp: "The mosques are our barracks, the domes our helmets, the minarets our bayonets, and the believers our soldiers" (Friedman, 2016). While the Turkish justice later released Erdoğan from jail and permitted him to go back to politics, the event signified a growing restlessness among the Kemalist secular elite and in the Turkish military.

The decade also brought challenges for Gülen in the form of health issues and legal battles. While living in the United States, in 2001, the Turkish state under the coalition government led by Democratic Left Party issued two warrants for his arrest that went into trial. Gülen was accused of establishing an illegal Islamist organization to destroy the secular Turkish state. Harrington (2011) best describes the circumstances surrounding the Gülen trial, noting:

> It is in this milieu of the country's judicial system that the Gülen trial unfolds: a prosecutor with unbridled discretion to file an indictment and begin a criminal trial in a State Security Court, under the watchful eye of the military, based on an extraordinarily broad definition of "terrorism" that encompassed political thought alone, in a judicial structure in which both the prosecutor and judges were appointed by a closed selection system, characterized by its ideological belief. (p. 68)

Gülen was residing in the U.S. at the time and did not go back to Turkey for trials; his attorneys represented him in the Turkish courts. Gülen knew that he would be in danger if he returned to Turkey and the U.S. was a safe(r) harbor. Gülen was acquitted of all charges in Turkish courts (Gülen v. K.H., 2006). In the wake of the trial, Gülen, now in the U.S., lived "a reclusive life reputedly characterised by religious asceticism" (Tee, p. 146) with a green card. Free from the reach of the Turkish courts controlled by at first the secular Turkish state and later by the Erdoğan regime, he chose the community of Saylorsburg, Pennsylvania, making the U.S. his permanent home.

The Ergenekon Case

However, despite being separated by oceans and continents, the hand of Turkish politics would continue to reach into the lives of Gülen, his followers, and the HM. In 2007, during the search of a house, the Turkish police unearthed a clandestine and illegal organization called Ergenekon (name of a myth explaining the origin of Turks). The massive network included politicians, lawyers, academics, journalists, generals and other high ranking military officers conspiring to overthrow Erdoğan's JDP government. The allegations against the Ergenekon network also included "attacks against minority groups, bombing mosques, assassinating public figures, blowing up a newspaper..." (Gürsoy, 2015, p. 104). The case surrounding the Ergenekon coup plot eventually came to be known as the Balyoz or Sledgehammer operation.

Many individuals, including current and former high-ranking military officers were arrested, tried, and convicted. In a protest against Erdoğan's JDP government's actions, in 2011, a number of generals resigned from their positions. However, the ultimatums and resignations from the generals and other high-rank officials did not create the effect those military officials were hoping for on the JDP government and the Turkish public and, for the first time in the Turkish Republic's history, the military lost its grip on power. Konda Research and Consultancy (2016) conducted a survey and found that "although 5 years ago, one in three people considered the armed forces as a source of pride, this rate has fallen below 10 percent after July 15th" (p. 70).

Ironically, all accused suspects and convicts were later freed and absolved of any charges. Many of these individuals ended up taking up positions in the very same government that had put them in jail, remaining to this very day in the current JDP government. Eventually, the planned coup to overthrow the government was dismissed as fabricated news altogether.

Nevertheless, the case still worked in favor of JDP to strengthen its regime. In the short run, it helped them harness the Kemalist military elite and establish stronger control over the military. In the long run, they used it to demonize HM in the public eye.

Perhaps the Sevres Syndrome, a common belief among Turkish people, has enabled the government to better manipulate Ergenekon for its own interests. The belief originates from the Treaty of Sevres the Ottoman Empire had signed after it was defeated by the allied forces—Great Britain, France, and Russia—in 1920. The treaty literally dissected the whole empire into little bits and left the Turkish nation with only a small piece of land in central Anatolia.

This caused a century-long national trauma and created a distrust towards anyone who was not Turkish. The syndrome professed itself in the treatment of minorities such as Jews, Armenians, Greeks, Kurds, and, more recently, the Syrian refugees. People came to believe that all the tensions and conflicts created in the country were the works of external forces. Populist politicians and governments later used this deep-rooted belief to their advantage and blamed the CIA, MOSSAD, MI6 and the likes as the sole instigators and conspirators of any unrest. The syndrome led to common—and derogatory—sayings such as "Only a Turk can be the true friend of another Turk," "(They) divide, disperse, and rule," "If you are a Turk, show it and make them shrink." As a result, both the pro-western secular military and Mr. Gülen in the U.S. fell prey to the regime. The HM leader, among many other things, was accused of being a CIA agent, a MOSSAD agent, and a secret Christian working for the Vatican by the pro-government media in Turkey.

HM Expands Operations

Still, the new millennium witnessed substantial growth, resulting in an influx of HM schools and institutions: new private schools, universities, and interfaith organizations were founded on almost all continents. The first Turkish Olympiads, later renamed as the International Festival of Language and Culture (IFLC), was held in 2003. As of 2021, ILFC became "an annual celebration of language diversity that showcases talent…" from over 160 countries (International Festival of Language & Culture, 2016). The HM also expanded its higher education initiatives to the USA. The North American University, first founded as The North American College in 2007, was "granted Bachelor and Master degrees through December 2017 by THECB and ACICS" (North American University, 2020).

However, advances in educational outreach were accompanied by its own issues. On a larger scale, the HM schools' emphasis and performance on humanities and social sciences has been poor. While Mr. Gülen mentioned several times that the new millennium could be characterized as an "Age of Social Sciences," the general focus in HM schools has historically been on STEM.

The 2010s: HM Starts Shrinking

A Downward Journey

In 2013, the tense relations between the HM and the JDP became even more strained. A significant event for this was the Gezi Park protests. The government wanted to demolish Gezi Park, a popular hangout spot and one of the few remaining green spaces in Taksim, Istanbul area, for commercial purposes. This was met with resistance and "the protesters opposed the demolition of the park for commercial purposes; in other words, they opposed the conversion of the park, a public space, into a private place" (Özen, 2015, p. 540). The JDP government responded harshly that later led the protests turn into a small-scale civil rights movement. The HM media did not back the Erdoğan administration's position. Hence, they grew apart. Shortly afterwards, what became known as the 17/25 December corruption case emerged and,—literally—all hell broke loose.

In 2013, the Turkish police conducted two criminal investigations on 17 and 25 December respectively and detained high-ranking politicians in the JDP government, accusing them of bribery, corruption, and fraud. This did not sit well with Erdoğan's cabinet, and they held the HM responsible. The JDP and the HM grew further apart. Erdoğan's cabinet soon began to interfere with HM institutions and their operations. Anyone remotely connected with the HM became a target as well. The government issued an arrest warrant for Mr. Gülen in November 2015 (Kaplan & Öztürk, 2015). Next, it seized Bank Asya in May 2015 (Karanfil, 2015). After that, the confiscation of Kaynak Holding and its subsidiaries followed, and a conservator was appointed in November 2015 (Kınık, 2015). A prominent HM figure and the CEO of Samanyolu Broadcasting Group (SBG), Hidayet Karaca, was arrested in December 2014 (Demirel, 2014). His lawyer, Gültekin Avcı, was jailed in September 2015 as well (Atik, 2015). Hidayet Karaca was later acquitted but not released. The judges who acquitted him were arrested in May 2015 (Usta, 2015). Operations continued and the state issued an arrest warrant for Zaman Newspaper's former chief editor, Ekrem Dumanli, in December 2015 (Koçak & Kılıç, 2015). Lucrative businesses sympathetic to HM were seized, too. The JDP government appointed a conservator in October 2015 to İpek Koza Holding and its subsidiaries (Kılıç & Koçak, 2015). Amsterdam and Partners LLP, a London-based law firm, was hired in order "to expose allegedly unlawful conduct by the Gülen network worldwide" (Pamuk, 2015). The officials arrested many more anti-JDP journalists such as Mehmet Baransu, Can Dündar, and Erdem Gül. Large-scale businesses close to HM such as Naksan Holding and Boydak Holding were seized. Eventually, Turkey's largest newspaper and HM's main media outlet, the Zaman newspaper was taken over in March 2016 (Kazancı, 2016). Government-owned and operated newspapers also published fabricated news stating Mr. Gülen was a freemason ("İşte Fethullah Gülen'in Masonluk belgeleri," 2015), which the Freemasons Lodge of Turkey immediately rejected (Dönmez, 2015).

There was an intermission in turmoil when some pro-HM representatives resigned from their positions within the JDP government. Since then, the movement has been declared the enemy of the state for not conforming to the harsh actions and retaliation. President Erdoğan publicly declared that the HM was, amongst many other things, "a parallel state, traitors, pawns of a dirty international blood lobby, they are a virus, tumour, blood-sucking leeches, terrorists, raving 'Hashashins,' assassins, they work with Mossad" and that actions against the HM was an independence war for all. He publicly promised to exterminate the whole movement ("Demonizing the Hizmet Movement," 2015, p. 2).

The Failed 2016 Coup and Its Aftermath

The Failed Military Coup

About three years after the 17/25 December corruption scandal, Turkey witnessed yet another military coup attempt on July 15, 2016. However, this unsuccessful overthrow was peculiar from the very beginning. Historically, military coups in Turkey occur in the early hours of the morning. Typically, the military first takes the president, the prime minister, and all other ministers and key personnel within the civilian government into custody. After securing the state, TV stations would then be taken over. The public is usually informed only after the coup attempt is fully complete and successful. On July 15, 2016, the attempted coup was not executed in that order.

The Unfolding of the Failed Coup

The failed coup started as a secret "non-conventional drill" (SCF, 2017, p. 20). On July 15 at 2:20 p.m., a military major officer went to the Turkish intelligence agency's office in Ankara and tipped them off regarding the nature of the event (p. 24). Hakan Fidan, head of Turkish intelligence, knew by 4:20 p.m. that a coup attempt was in progress, yet did not inform state officials regarding the conflict. The general public knew of the attempt around 8:00 p.m. when the military started blocking the roads leading to the Bosphorus Bridge. Eventually, guards only granted one-way access to the bridge around 10:00 p.m. on July 15. In the meantime, President Erdoğan left his vacation home in Marmaris, a small vacation town in southwest Turkey by the Aegean coast and got on the presidential plane. While on the plane, he connected to CNN Türk and asked the public to get out onto the streets and resist. He blamed the HM as the plotter. Around 2:40 a.m. on July 16, military planes bombed the Turkish parliament. Forty minutes later, around 3:20 a.m., the presidential plane landed at İstanbul Atatürk Airport. Putschists, who the president claimed to be HM participants, released General Hulusi Akar, chief of military general staff, around 8:30 a.m.. The coup attempt was over by early afternoon on July 16 (pp. 10–11).

Stockholm Center for Freedom's (SCF) report (2017) claims the coup attempt was staged and bases the claim on several factors: (i) President Erdoğan's conflicting remarks about his whereabouts on that day; (ii) Hakan Fidan, head of Turkish intelligence wasn't asked to resign, nor testify; (iii) the military officers who spent a great deal of effort to suppress the coup attempt were later dismissed from the military; and, (iv) no autopsies were conducted on the 249 Turkish citizens who died that day (p. 16).

In the immediate aftermath, Mr. Gülen denied any involvement in the coup and issued a statement where he condemned in the

> strongest terms, the attempted military coup in Turkey. Government should be won through a process of free and fair elections, not force. I pray to God for Turkey, for Turkish citizens, and for all those currently in Turkey that this situation is resolved peacefully and quickly. (Alliance for Shared Values, 2016, July 15)

After news surfaced in the western media that some Gülen sympathizers might have been involved in the coup attempt, he clarified his stance further and stated that "if I were to even entertain that idea, if anyone among those soldiers had called me and told me of their plan, I would have told them, you are committing murder" (Gulen, 2017).

The Aftermath of the Failed Coup

Regardless, the impact of the failed coup on the HM was disastrous. In Turkey, the government closed 180 media outlets, 1,254 non-profit organizations, and 2,099 schools and dormitories. 120 journalists, 5,266 military officers, and 159 high ranking generals were arrested. Moreover, 346 academics and 3,465 judges and prosecutors were dismissed from their positions. Altogether, 50,651 people were detained. In sum, over 100,000 people were directly affected ("The failed military coup," 2016, pp. 12–13).

Outside Turkey, in an effort to interfere with HM operations outside Turkey, Erdoğan's JDP government established the Maarif Foundation in 2016. On their website, the organization states that the "Turkish Maarif Foundation serves as a gateway to international educational arena of Turkish that will contribute to enhancing cultural and civilizational interaction and paving the way for achieving the common wellbeing. " (The Maarif Foundation, 2023a). Soon after its foundation, Maarif "took over 32 FETO-affiliated schools in Somali, Guinea, Niger, Sudan and Republic of the Congo, in its very first years, and it started educational activities in the standards of Maarif Foundation in these countries." (The Maarif Foundation, 2023b). The foundation also "signed protocols with Pakistan, Ethiopia, Gambia, Sierra Leone, Burkina Faso, Burundi, Djibouti, Chad, Gabon, Cameroon, Madagascar, Mali, Mauretania, Senegal, and Democratic Republic of Sao Tome and Principe…" (2023b) to transfer HM schools over to Maarif.

While Turkey drifted into chaos, the government declared a state of emergency. Amnesty International's annual report on human rights revealed the grave situation. According to the report (2017), 118 journalists were in pre-trial detention, and 184 media outlets and 375 NGOs, including women's rights groups, lawyers' associations, and humanitarian organizations, were shut down by executive decree. The state increased Internet restrictions, the police used excessive force and tortured, and ill-treated people they detained. They also restricted detainee access to lawyers (pp. 368–369). The numbers include all HM institutions as well. At this point, it is safe to state that no HM-related businesses or institutions exist in Turkey. A couple of days before the first anniversary of the staged coup attempt, the Turkish Minister of Justice Bekir Bozdağ stated that 168,801 people had undergone legal action, 615 people had been under custody, and 8,069 people had been issued arrest warrants since July 15, 2016. He also added that 50,504 people had been arrested and 48, 371 people were on parole for HM-related legal actions. ("Bakan Bozdağ," 2017).

Following the failed coup attempt in 2016, President Erdoğan added the acronym FETÖ (Fethullah Terror Organization) to his repertoire. After declaring a state of emergency and decrees with the force of law in July 2016, the Turkish Government took measures that included,

> The outright dismissal of a large number of civil servants, as well as the dissolution and seizure of assets of non-governmental organisations or other private entities (media, schools, hospitals, etc.), either by adding their names to lists appended to such decrees or by empowering administrative authorities to do so through simplified procedures. (Mijatović, 2020, pp. 21–22)

On a side note, Reza Zarrab, the main actor behind the initial corruption charges, was arrested on March 19, 2016, in Miami, FL. He was charged with circumventing "U.S. sanctions by conducting millions of dollars-worth of transactions on behalf of the Iranian government and Iranian businesses" ("Turkish national arrested," 2016). He later went to trial and confessed his wrongdoings.

President Erdoğan later called the coup attempt "a gift from God" (p. 6).
In the meantime, the witch-hunt is still on.

· 3 ·
THE PHILOSOPHY

Gülenian Philosophy on Education and HM Schools

I was lucky enough to secure a personal interview with Mr. Gülen and hear directly from him what he perceived education to be. I first start with a short account of my observations of the location to set the context, and then move on to details from the interview as well as information I compiled from other sources regarding his philosophy of education. I also present themes I created as a result of the interview and research on the body of literature.

Researcher Meets Mentor

The interview took place in Gülen's home, located in a medium-sized town in the Appalachian Mountains. Upon entry into the building, I was welcomed by shoe racks that touched the ceiling of the small entryway on the first floor. In keeping with pre-Islamic tradition, many Turkish people take off their shoes when entering their homes; this place was no exception. After my own shoes found a space on the rack, I turned right and proceeded to a sunroom that had been reorganized as the dining commons. The windows from the three sides of the room let in the winter sun. A stairwell led up to the second floor to a large family room to the left-hand side. On the right, a series of doors loomed ahead on each side of the hallway.

The family room, like the rest of the building, was carpeted. People were sitting on the floor and on sleeper sofas with Turkish manufacturer labels. These sleeper sofas were lined up against the walls; the only other furniture in the room were small coffee tables. The style and arrangement were reminiscent of the dershane or light house apartment from my youth in Turkey. The furnishing was adopted for two reasons: first, simplicity in decor was considered a sign of humility and frugality. Second, the large empty center of the living room or salon served as a space to conduct prayers, five times a day. The purpose of this ritual was to tighten the ties of brotherhood and ensure a common routine.

As I peered into the big room, a group of men—no women were present—were reading books. Islamic calligraphy hanging on the walls displayed the ninety-nine attributes of Allah and the name of the Prophet Mohammad. Since portraits are generally prohibited in Islamic art, the bold script was commonly used as artwork in HM homes. The family room faced the driveway and parking lot down below. Hardwood windows with white frames invited in the sunshine.

An additional flight of stairs led up to a locked door on the third floor that served as Gülen's living quarters. At certain times of the day, the stairs were frequented by men hoping the door would be unlocked so the guests could enter their esteemed scholar's private domain. Occasionally, select visitors who were admitted were able to pray with him; ask questions; and listen to the imam's talks. Having finally been granted permission, I ascended the stairway to the third floor. With a slight knock on the door, I was poised to meet the leader of the HM in person whose philosophy had impressed me as a student, teacher, and researcher.

When I first entered his living quarters, the imam was sitting in an armchair. A small coffee table was positioned at his right-hand side with a glass of water, his medications, and a book. Two young visitors sat on their heels on the floor, talking to him. They looked to be in their twenties. From the way the youth were dressed, I deducted they were either his students or observant Muslims. The young men, departed soon afterwards, and we were left alone.

Unsure of protocol, I did not know where to sit, so I followed suit and sat on my heels on the floor. After introducing myself, Gülen noted that sitting on the floor in such a manner might hurt my knees and invited me to join him on the sofa right next to his armchair. When I later pondered this action, I thought that he must have been informed I was an academic, and as an academic, he elevated me to his own level. This way, he showed that education was his priority.

A soft-spoken individual, the humble leader showed great respect for his visitors. He also exuded charisma. When the interview started, I wasn't nervous. However, I was unsure if the esteemed Muslim cleric would judge my looks, language, or demeanor. For example, my dyed black hair was frowned upon within conservative circles. I also wondered how much time I would have with Gülen. It was customary for people to wait for months to speak with him for only a few minutes. The interview evolved into a longer conversation than I expected without any kind of rush. He was extremely polite and attentive to my questions, resulting in a delightful experience. I was able to ask him about the state of education and inquire regarding home language use and bilingual education.

In order to conduct the interview, I agreed to honor a few conditions when cultivating the fruit of our exchange. Therefore, while the following account relates Gülen's thoughts from our interview, it is important that the reader understand the corpus of the content was shaped in a collaborative process. As such, the passages below were derived from a compilation of my own initial interview notes; the correction and expansion of these comments by a trusted colleague of Gülen; direct quotes from our conversation; and excerpts derived from his many writings.

Principles of Gülenian Educational Philosophy

The present-day HM is a global initiative dedicated to the well-being of humankind through quality education. While Gülen had written many books and lectured on various subjects, the topic of education was of high priority for him. Gülen's philosophy ascertained that the role of education—as an essential social institution—was to generate various mechanisms in humans that led them to do good works for humanity. The schools established under his guidance affirmed this commitment. He noted in the interview, "The only means that will lead the human being into divine wisdom and have him serve the common good is education that starts in the family and continues in the society."

Once Gülen started answering my questions, I was seized with a sudden moment of understanding that we were in accord. My body, mind, and heart felt and believed there should be more to schools and education. Schools must serve as catalysts for an equitable and just society. They must go beyond developing the cognitive skills of students with positive sciences; they must deconstruct the desensitized and white-washed norms and behaviors so that there is room for social-emotional practices, and aesthetic education.

Scholars who studied Gülen's educational philosophy express similar opinions. For example, Çelik (2010) characterizes the implementation of this philosophy as a pedagogical approach dictated by four educational values, including: an appreciation for learning; altruism; a tripartite relationship between students, teachers, and families; and the integration of science and religion (pp. 98–105).

Also, while HM schools were initially rooted in the Sufi Islamic tradition, Alam (2019) emphasizes that, "Gulen's educational discourse fundamentally differs from the approach of the late nineteenth-twentieth century model of Islamic modernism" (p. 166). On close inspection, the foundational principles of a Gülenian educational philosophy mirror progressive ideals reflected in the history of American education, including cultural competence, diversity, equity, and inclusion.

Education as a Process of Unification

Gülenian philosophy rests on the core principle that education is a fundamental, lifelong process of unification. For example, education connects childhood with adulthood in physical and psychological spaces to prepare novice for expertise. HM educators place the dialectical unification of student, teacher, and family at the heart of their approach. This bridge between home and school integrates the individual with society through developmental processes balancing high morals with scientific knowledge.

The fundamental concept of unification distinguishes HM's enduring commitment to education, regardless of the belief systems of students, faculty, or administrators. Indeed, Gülen's Islamic religious tradition harbors, "no necessary contradiction between science and religion", uniting peoples, faiths, and academic disciplines (Yavuz, 2013, p. 92). As Yavuz (2013) stated, "Education, for Gülen, is not about affirming one tradition and identity in opposition to another, but rather teaching in a way to indicate their connections and similarities, and the fact that the crisis of modernity or post-modernity and the search for meaning and solidarity is shared by all human communities" (p. 108).

Hence, Gülen's unifying goal for HM schools is not to teach religion in schools or modernize Islam via education. Rather, education is considered a complex socialization process that is "bottom-up, moral, and ethical, rather than technical, and concerned with the inculcation of universal values … and ethics of social responsibility and individual accountability" (Alam, 2019, p. 169). In this manner, "education for Gulen is a "totalizing discourse," concerned with the moral and ethical regeneration of human societies" (Alam, 2019, p. 179).

A Focus on Humanity

As a process of unification, Gülenian educational philosophy focuses on the development of human beings. Gülen contends that all human beings are fundamentally the children of a Supreme Deity, deserving to "reside in the kingdom of heaven". Individually and collectively, human beings consist of a "tripartite division" between the heart or spirit; head or mind; and hands or habit, also referred to as the body or character (Çelik, 2010, p. 101).

According to Gülen, students naturally possess "seeds of goodness"—including perception, emotions, and thoughts—and are considered good by nature. Education offers the means by which these perceptual, emotional, and cognitive assets are fed, watered, and nurtured into positive human potential. He asserts the teacher's responsibility is to educate the student in all three areas. Through the process of education, schools and systems protect the conscience of children and help them to flourish in accordance with the spirit that resides within them.

A summary of Gülenian principles ascertains that, as an essential social institution, the role of education is to promote human development, interfaith dialogue, and universal peace by generating various mechanisms that lead human beings to do good works for humanity. By placing individual human beings front and center, the conditions, nature, and future of humanity as a larger whole are impacted. As Çelik (2010) notes, the process of education can then provide solutions to social problems "such as terror, anarchy, and conflict. Mr. Gülen has the conviction that these problems can only be overcome with knowledge (through education), work capital (through labor) and unification (through dialogue)" (p. 99).

Mission of Development

In focusing on humanity, HM educators are motivated by a mission dedicated to the growth of all individuals, families, and communities, ensuring the progress of the larger human family. As a result, HM schools are unique in their commitment to provide a quality education for under-served students who might not otherwise have the opportunity to experience academic rigor nor become equipped with the highest qualifications while "bound by virtues". The mission of HM schools provides the vehicle by which this essential need can be met regardless of wealth, ability, race, or religion. Stand-alone institutions and school networks that follow Gülenian principles meet and fulfill the mission of preserving and nurturing the child's potential.

Pedagogy as a Balanced Approach to Learning and Development

The term pedagogy is used to describe how educators employ specific methods and practices that promote learning to occur. Interestingly, a Gülenian approach does not adopt or advocate on behalf of particular forms of classroom instruction. As Gage (2014) states, Gülen "has not addressed himself specifically to pedagogy and curriculum, but generally a holistic approach to life, of which education is an inseparable component" (p. 17).

Instead, Gülen regards education as a means to improve a child's moral strengths in tandem with scientific knowledge. HM educators from the study concurred with this vision, noting "education should appeal to their hearts, not only for their brains". To meet this end, HM educators apply his principles as a philosophical template or general guide, while sifting this balanced approach to learning and development through the rules, regulations, and practices of the countries in which they serve.

Curriculum as the Reflective, Contextualized, Lived Experience

While pedagogies refer to how to implement the teaching-learning process, curriculums establish what is taught or learned. HM schools deliberately teach content like science, math, and other subject areas; additionally, Gülenian educational philosophy aims to develop students' moral dimensions through a living curriculum. By awakening students' understandings of universal values including acceptance, broad-mindedness, tolerance, dialogue, and respect, HM schools cultivate unity and the physical, mental, and emotional spaces in which teaching-learning opportunities can occur.

The curriculum has long been a focal point in the history of American education. What we teach forms the basis of our syllabi, use of instructional time, target outcomes, and performance expectations of students. As a historical-political, sociocultural construct, today's curriculum became an area of scholarly interest during the Progressive movement, when educators sought to institutionalize features of what students learn in school (Flinders & Thornton, 2017, p. 1). Prominent educators from the era included John Dewey, Maria Montessori, Jane Adams, and Franklin Bobbitt.

Due to the "organic connection between education and personal experience" (Dewey, 1997, p. 25), Dewey ascertained schools needed "a philosophy of education based upon a philosophy of experience" (p. 29). Therefore, the great American philosopher advocated for connected, interesting, and motivating experiences in schools that were also authentic with concrete outcomes (p. 26). Dewey maintained that these experiences should not be exclusively reserved for the subject-matter taught. Instead, he highlighted educators' responsibility and power to provide students experiences in collateral learning based on objective conditions. The American educational philosopher asserted collateral learning led to the "formation of enduring attitudes, of likes and dislikes... and is much more important than the spelling lesson or lesson in geography or history" (p. 48). Without such collateral learning experiences, Dewey asserted that "the individual loses his own soul: loses appreciation of things worthwhile, of values to which these things are relative" (p. 49).

Similarly, Gülenian educational philosophy does not view schools as places where the curriculum is simply transmitted as information or a capitalistic commodity to students. Indeed, Gülen would agree that a primary responsibility of educators is that they not only be aware of the general principle of the shaping of actual experience by environing conditions, but that they also recognize in the concrete what surroundings are conducive to having experiences that lead to growth. (Dewey, 1997, p. 40).

In emphasizing curriculum as the reflective, contextualized lived experience, Gage (2014) identifies Dewey and Gülen as the grandfathers that inspired the wisdom movement (p. 29). This initiative aims to transform the curriculum in three ways. First, members seek to liberate the curriculum from a restricted "transmission of established facts and job training skills only…[to] the generation of life through authentic, meaningful aesthetic transactions and the acquisition of wisdom" (p. 29). Second, the wisdom movement seeks to refocus the curriculum on "human language, artistic expression of cross-cultural fluencies, and character development in addition to science education" (p. 29). Finally, the wisdom movement seeks to implement a curriculum that engages the individual in civic and community engagement to generate "a citizenry for voluntary cooperative undertakings" (p. 29). Indeed, excellence in HM schools was attributed to a focus on curriculum as the reflective, contextualized, and lived experience of moral education, culture, and the STEM courses educators taught.

Teachers as Soul Engineers

The role of the teacher in Gülenian philosophy cannot be underestimated. While the tripartite relationship is organized in the relationship between the "educator, the parents, and the sponsor for the altruistic service" (Çelik, 2010, p. 101), educators are distinguished as catalysts of the educational process or "soul engineers" as described by Gülen himself.

The metaphor of teachers as soul engineers runs through the notion of light houses as places where HM educators improve their character, learn high moral values, and challenge their intellect "where same-sex roommates from different social and economic backgrounds live in a culture of harmony, brotherhood, and spirituality, provide a clean and safe alternative for university students from socially and politically conservative and/or insecure milieus in Turkey" (Yavuz, 2013, p. 100). According to Gülenian educational philosophy, the road that leads to a soul engineer title runs through the light houses.

Across the study presented in this book, the teachers' love for their students, subject matter, and profession were identified as being essential to achieving the mission, implementing content and context-specific pedagogies, and nurturing understandings. These professional competencies are equally esteemed by the active expression of their own cultural values, moral qualities, and commitment to being role models. Interviews across the study consistently pointed to the principle that teachers are a school's greatest asset and, in the case of HM's educational objectives, were squarely responsible for students' and schools' success.

HM teachers demonstrate altruism in education in a variety of ways, including financial sacrifice, the provision of time, and accessibility. Indeed, many dedicated HM educators place their students before their own financial interests. As a Gülenian principle, the value of altruism places "the focus is on example (temsil), not on preaching (tebliğ)" (Çelik, 2010, p. 100). In this manner, teachers actively embody the reflective, lived curriculum, demonstrating "values such as truthfulness, trust, respect for parents, respect for the elderly, respect for one's heritage, and love for human beings" (p. 100) through their very own daily interactions with students.

Indeed, educators' time and energy to bridge home and school into every aspect of the learners' lives offers ethical, esteemed, and available adults for students to actively emulate. HM educators typically see education as a form of prayer, and therefore consider unpaid, overtime hours as an investment. The antecedent for this mindset comes from the Quran where the first command God gave to the Muslims was "to read." The Prophet Muhammad also stated, "when a man dies, his acts come to an end, but three, recurring charity, or knowledge [by which people] benefit, or a pious son, who prays for him" ("Abu Huraira (Allah be pleased with him) reported Allah's messenger", 2017). Knowledge, in this case, represents education as a positive, enduring act to carry out. Ali and other prominent historical religious figures noted they would be "a slave" to anyone for forty years, or a long time, if they taught him a new word.

In today's society, these metaphorical assertions remain deeply embedded in the consciousness of Muslims. While secular in curriculum and practice, teachers' spiritual intentions employ education as a medium to reach God. Sadly, the notion can lead HM educators to extremes, neglecting their health, personal lives, and families. This unhealthy dynamic is observed when educators teach students all day, conduct evening and weekend student tutoring, visit students' families during personal time, coach science Olympiad teams, and prepare lessons until dawn every day of the week.

In the last analysis, a Gülenian philosophy of education calls for an active system of human beings dedicated to each other in "a learning circle that consists of family, school, friends, neighbors, faith, and cultural organizations, and workplaces". Educational systems that seek to support and develop their students not only benefit the student and educator, but contribute to families, communities, and the larger society. However, for Gülen, "what matters most is [not] the secular orientation and physical space of the educational institution but the "cognitive map" of the teacher who interacts with and retains the power of transmitting knowledge and value to students" (Alam, 2019, p. 180).

· 4 ·

THE PEDAGOGY AND THE INTERVIEWS

My Teaching Experience and HM Educator Interviews

I had experienced Gülenian philosophy as a student and teacher on two different continents within diverse historical-political conditions and sociocultural contexts. After my interview with Gülen, I set out to see how his educational beliefs were reflected on yet another continent as an educational researcher. What did Hizmet schools look like across the United States? Did HM educators perceive and translate Gülen's beliefs? As members of a trans-national, educational movement, what could the U.S. educational system learn from HM schools?

The first part of this chapter provides context by presenting my experiences and observations in HM schools as a teacher. After this background information, the chapter presents findings from interviews conducted with eight educators associated with private HM schools in the U.S. Although eight interviews took place, five of them are reported here to keep the context cohesive. All the interviewees were college-educated, Turkish males and fluent speakers in both English and Turkish. The majority of the educators were administrators between thirty and fifty years old. Most of the schools were located in and around large metropolitan cities in the Midwest, with one boarding school in a small town on the east coast. These HM charter schools were typically operating within non-descript buildings without many outward signs of the school's existence.

Thick descriptions in the ethnographic account below provide an account of the site, individual, and beliefs of key personnel associated with each school. The reader will additionally note that data was collected with interviewees serving the HM movement at a variety of levels within the U.S. network. The descriptive portraits account for unique and common themes of each pedagogical constituent in relationship to the interviewees' perceptions on Gülenian philosophy and education.

My Experiences as a Teacher in HM Schools

Organizational Structures of HM Uzbek-Turkish Schools

In Uzbekistan, HM schools consisted of two dimensions distinguished by the nationality of the teachers: Teachers from Turkey provided instruction in biology, chemistry, English, math, physics, computer science, and Turkish, while their local partners taught history, geography, language and literature, art and physical education in the local language. Although this linguistic separation would not be considered ideal practice by bilingual education scholars today, the organizational structures proved to be a selling point at the time. And it worked.

With the exception of the elementary grades, the HM schools in Central Asia were all-boys' or all-girls' schools. The Turkish school personnel consisted of Turkish and local males and females, HM administrators, and HM teachers. The girls' schools were staffed with administrators and teachers who were mostly Muslim HM females. In time, a teacher shortage grew exponentially, resulting in efforts to employ some non-HM personnel from Turkey. However, because of distance and low wages, this effort was short-lived.

To gain entry into secondary studies, high school candidates took entrance exams. Upon admission, the adolescents wore uniforms, lived in school dorms for the most part, and attended *etudes* or evening study sessions monitored by teachers. Previously, the etudes were part of a *belletmen*, or mentors, job. However, because of political tensions between Turkey and Uzbekistan at the time and other reasons, the *belletmen* did not monitor students anymore in my school.

A school day consisted of eight hours of instruction with a lunch break after the fifth period. Students were loaned books that needed to be returned in clean condition at the end of the school year. The English as a second language texts came with teacher guides. I placed the teacher's manual in front of me while teaching and followed the instructions diligently. Most of my colleagues and I did not possess any pedagogical background, so the teacher guides were lifesavers.

The students almost always had homework which was assigned from workbooks. Assessment was generally implemented in the form of multiple-choice tests which were a tradition reminiscent of the Turkish teachers' educational backgrounds. Every Monday morning before school started,—and Friday afternoons before the two-day weekend break—, the whole school sang both the Uzbek and Turkish national anthems in the schoolyard. Both a Turkish and an Uzbek principal made important announcements at that time as well.

SILM Headquarters and Pedagogical "Unplanning"

SILM, a central administration office in the capital city oversaw the running of the school system. The building was also a place where meetings between state officials were held, and subject area department heads were positioned. These department heads would create new instructional materials and assessment methods; organize professional development sessions for teachers during school breaks; and serve as points of contact between the central administration and school personnel who were mostly novice and young teachers.

Despite the weak economy in post-Soviet era Uzbekistan, the dedication of attentive teachers, strict discipline, rigorous curriculum, and motivated students resulted in educational success. Today, as an education professor at a U.S. university, I know now that many of my HM colleagues were not properly trained in effective curriculum planning, instructional methods, classroom management strategies, assessment tools, culturally appropriate instruction, or state standards. At some point, we were supposed to write lesson plans, but that requirement quickly disappeared. The practice was perceived as a burden and, since most of the teachers were there on a voluntary basis and were paid a minimal $300 single rate to $500 family rate a month, professional development and lesson planning was and could not be enforced.

HM Schools in Turkey vs. Uzbekistan

The HM schools in Turkey were private schools; they were not run by the state. They were still inspected by the state; however, the schools had a certain level of autonomy. Student demographics in Turkey differed from those in Uzbekistan and Indonesia where the majority of the students came from working class families. In contrast, students in the private HM school experienced the privileges and benefits associated with middle- and upper-class families.

Regardless of their private or public status, all K-12 schools in Turkey were required to adopt the Turkish Ministry of Education's curriculum and were subject to state inspection. Private schools hired their own personnel, while state schools implemented a centralized teacher placement system with what was distinguished as "mandatory eastern service". At the time, the cities in eastern Turkey were engaged in a period of economic development; personnel in medical, legal, and educational professions including doctors, police officers, and teachers were required to serve a certain time-period, typically between 3 and 7 years to maintain their state teaching license and benefits. Private school teachers were waived from this requirement, but those educators who desired a state teaching license needed to work at a state school in east Turkey complete this compulsory service.

While the mandatory medium of instruction was Turkish, both state and private schools were allowed to teach in English, German, and French as second languages. Other languages, including Arabic, Kurdish, Yiddish, and Armenian were negatively viewed and explicitly banned as a mother tongue or first language in schools. Toward this end, Article 42 on Right and Duty of Training and Education in the Constitution of the Republic of Turkey (TBMM) (1982) notes:

> No language other than Turkish shall be taught as a mother tongue to Turkish citizens at any institution of education. Foreign languages to be taught in institutions of education and the rules to be followed by schools conducting education in a foreign language shall be determined by law. The provisions of international treaties are reserved. (TBMM, 1982, p. 20)

A typical school day was similar to schools in Uzbekistan and Indonesia, consisting of eight hours of instruction with a lunch break after the fifth period. In the private school in which I worked; students were also required to wear uniforms. Families purchased uniforms and school supplies from their own resources. Unlike the institutions in Uzbekistan and Indonesia, Turkish HM schools were co-educational with both girls and boys sharing the same classroom.

The student population enrolled in my private high school consisted of three cohorts. All cohorts were housed inside the same building. Incoming students were placed according to their performance on middle and high school entrance tests conducted by the Turkish Department of Education. Students placed in the lower cohort, the General High School, received a traditional high school curriculum with a focus on general education.

The mid-level cohort was an Anatolian High School. This institution was a more selective school where the medium of instruction was mostly English. The third cohort, the Science High School, was the most selective school with a rigorous STEM curriculum. Students in this school had a record of getting high scores in the college entrance exams and represented the crème de la crème of all students. They also competed in the local and global Science Olympiads, and eventually went on to attend Turkish and foreign Ivy League universities in Europe and the US.

Regardless of the type of private HM high school or cohort students were placed, all secondary freshman students were required to take a year-long English period. These three cohorts did not have different teachers; all teachers, including myself, taught all cohorts. However, depending on the cohort, the expectations were either high or low. The Turkish Department of Education standards were used to design the curriculum except English. In English, most teachers followed a teaching manual as an instructional guide. At the time, the Communicative Method (Nunan, 1991) was popular. As a result, students and teachers were put "an emphasis on learning to communicate through interaction in the target language" (Nunan, 1991, p. 279) in class.

Other subjects, including math, biology, and history focused on preparing students to take a centralized college exam administered by the Turkish Higher Education Council. Class sizes enrolled up to thirty students, resulting in chronic behavior management issues. Our assistant principal spent most of his time calling parents. Teachers were required to attend regular department meetings and professional development days across the school year as well.

HM Educator Interviews

Director of a Private, All-Boys' Secondary Boarding School on the East Coast

My first interview took place at a private, all-boys' secondary boarding school in a small, middle-class town on the East Coast in the U.S. With a population of 122 students, a little over half the student body was comprised of international youth from various countries. As I made my way onto the school grounds, I observed some students heading towards a school building with classrooms despite the fact it was Sunday. A detached, two-story colonial building with dark red brick walls stood out from the northwest side of the school, offering dorm housing for all of the students. The roof, protected by black asphalt, tar shingles stretched down to freshly painted, white gutters. Seven white, double windows facing out from the second floor echoed by six symmetrical panes on the ground floor. A barrel-vaulted, solid canopy entrance replaced the seventh window in the middle. Steps led up to a pair of elevated, white wooden double doors.

Adjacent to the dormitory, in the middle of a well-kept lawn, a brown wooden sign sat in front of the building. Bright metal letters spelled out the school's name. A driveway around the lawn separated the grass from the dorm. I looked ahead and, once again, faced the two-story, mid-century school building. Its industrial design resonated to a bygone era. Later, I learned that the building had been built in 1962 and was used as a church, likely by Catholics as the choice denomination of the area.

The building, when first erected, was meant to be simple and integrated with nature, but its yellow enamel panels on metal walls and windows made it look out of place. The rest of the building facade was constructed of light cream-colored brick. Grey metal frames reached up to the flat roof, connected by exposed flashings that surrounded standard ribbon windows. The right side of the entrance housed an oval extension with stained windows that served as a chapel in its heyday but have since been designated as classrooms. Walking through the cement entryway and grey metal double doors, I entered an 8′–10′ foot, square-shaped room with windows, next to the main school entrance since opening in 2002.

The first thing that attracted my attention was the aquarium with goldfish and slightly blurry water. The tank was reminiscent of my experiences in the 1980s and 1990s when four to five students would be assigned to a *dersane* or light house. Students would put their money together and buy an aquarium with colorful creatures to beautify the barely furnished student homes. A samovar or tea maker was visible on a counter. A customary part of meals, conversations, visits, and all other occasions in Turkey, the tea provides evidence of an intergenerational ritual from my *dersane* days. We would get together in the evenings and read the *Risales*-Bediuzzaman or Said Nursi's books before bedtime. Tea was always served and, if our budget would allow it, be accompanied by petite beurre biscuits or sweet crackers.

Pictures of Istanbul and Turkey hung on the walls, possibly indicating the school director's longing for the motherland or serve as a reminder of his national affiliation across several continents. The room needs paint. The director offers me tea in a curved glass from Turkey; I observe a cultural attachment he is unwilling or unable to let go: Turkish tea must always be served in a curved Turkish tea glass, a delicate, hard-to-find item in the U.S. Before entering his personal office space, the principal engaged in a short conversation with an English-speaking, American teacher. Inside, we conduct the interview in Turkish. As a language specialist, I could tell his fluency in Turkish was more advanced than his fluency in English.

With a head of slightly greying and receding hair, the administrator looked to be in his early 40's. He was of medium build, with a fair skin tone, and stood at an average height. His clean shirt and neatly pressed trousers remind me of an era when all the *abis* or elder brothers would dress similarly to mimic Gülen. Back in the day, many HM followers emulated the imam unquestioningly, even down to the most striking detail of dismissing a tie. I have never seen Gülen wear a tie, although he claims otherwise. The absence of this formality was hype among HM followers for some time. The fad came and went, but the fashion sense of some administrators like this one seemed to linger in the past.

From my interview with the second participant, two themes strongly emerged regarding his perceptions of Gülenian educational philosophy. The first theme was that "tolerance promotes unity and creates better educational opportunities" while the second espoused the notion that "charter schools with HM educators carry out a great mission and are assets for education".

Theme: Tolerance, Unity, and Educational Opportunities

On several occasions during our discussion, the director commented on the unifying role of the school and how the principle of tolerance created an atmosphere that enabled students to live and work together. For example, he stated, "When you enter a room or a classroom, you can see [those] students with different skin colors, religions, and cultures. They respect each other in this educational environment." The principal noted that students in attendance represented diverse global and regional geographic areas, "from many different countries. They live here altogether."

Asserting tolerance as a mission of both the institution and Hizmet Movement, he emphasized the existence of acceptance and broad-mindedness as a crucial objective of the institution. The school director asserted, "Students, regardless of their backgrounds, beliefs and skin colors, respectfully share this educational environment with each other", making a clear reference to the importance of religious tolerance when stating "a student from a different denomination can freely express his thoughts without any reservations because people respect that."

Theme: The Mission and Assets of HM Charter Schools

According to the director, HM charter schools provide a quality education for a low-income population in need of academic rigor, commenting: "I see those charter schools as assets that support this particular population and doing a great job at it as well. I also see a good future ahead of them. Right now, they are filling a great void. They should be supported, and they should increase in number."

Later, he continued this same train of thought, noting that charter schools in general sought to address the needs of students with smaller classrooms and lower teacher-to-student ratios, suggesting, "In those charter schools, there is an effort to increase the achievement rate of students through individualized education programs in smaller classrooms and with more teachers per student." Moreover, he expressed the importance and role of HM educators in charter schools in their mission to provide students with the best education possible, remarking "charter schools address each child's needs, teachers there are caring, and they try to educate the students the best way they can. Thus, they get great results."

In general, during the interview, I sensed that the principal's opinion was that both private HM schools and charter schools with HM educators offered a positive approach as a new form of education. Finally, the school director prioritized instruction in English since the school was in the U.S.

Principal of a Private, Midwestern, PreK-8th HM Grade School

For my second interview, I traveled to a school situated in the suburbs of a large town in the U.S. Midwest. As I parked my car in the lot of an "L" shaped building, I noticed that there were few signs marking the presence of this private HM school. The school occupied only one side of the building, while the other housed a Christian charity. The irony of this juxtaposition reminded me of the tolerance of the Ottoman era when mosques and churches were built side by side. The PreK-8 school curriculum was based on developmental objectives in the lower grades, with a focus on mastering important academic skills in the upper grades. A typical school day ran from 8:20 a.m. to 3:55 p.m., with before and after-school care. The teacher-student ratio was capped at 1:20.

The sign in front of what appeared to be the main entrance did not indicate it was the correct way to enter the school. I pulled on the door and was not surprised to find it locked. The school secretary buzzed me into the reception area. Colorful, student artwork had been posted on walls of an otherwise plain, pale blue. The receptionist seemed to perform a multitude of jobs, including welcoming guests, serving as the principal's secretary; keeping track of attendance; and maintaining the security of the premises. Except for one or two children seated in the main office, everyone else was in class. Asking for the director's office, I was surprised to discover it was located right next to the secretary's space, divided only by two thin bookshelves. The principal's office was smaller than my own living room, at approximately seven by nine feet squared.

The principal was sitting at his desk, with his back facing a window. Rising, he stood up and welcomed me by shaking my hand, a common gesture between men in Turkey. Outside, a large lawnmower constantly produced noise throughout the duration of the interview. At one point, the mechanical buzzing disrupted the conversation, causing me to worry about transcribing the audio recording later into a transcription. The principal shared that he was a science major and had a college degree. He had a fuller figure; was of average height; and looked like he was in his early 30s with prematurely, balding, black hair. He was clean-shaven, wearing tan colored shirt and grey trousers. The calm and friendly expression on his face told me I was welcome in his school. Like the rest of the HM participants I interviewed in person, the principal is married to a woman.

The school director shared that he had the opportunity to travel to several countries as a result of various HM appointments. I was not surprised to hear this information, as a common practice in HM institutions. Occasionally, people are moved because of their circumstances including the need for medical care; the desire to pursue advanced education; or to staff key personnel in a new school. Other times a transfer takes place and individuals are moved simply because change is considered to be "good".

Because the principal was very articulate in English, we conducted the interview in English. He answered all the questions I posed with an open mind. Sometimes, HM participants adopt a *tedbir* or precautionary stance as a security measure. As a result, people in the movement can be extremely guarded situations, but I did not witness this reserve in him.

Theme: The Key to Success: Dedicated Hizmet Teachers

During this interview, a single theme emerged from our conversation that dedicated Hizmet teachers were the key to success. The administrator made it clear that he had strong faith in HM educators. On many occasions, he highlighted the importance of the human factor in education. He shared his impressions: "And the instructors…what I can say is their character, the instructor's character, the instructor's, you know… background is very important." More specifically, he spoke to their individual dedication to pedagogy: "So what I can say is from Hizmet point of view, those educators care, they love the kids, and try to help those kids because I have seen teachers that they were working up to 3 a.m. and then just study for their classes the next day." He continued adding: "What runs the system is actually human beings."

As he concluded his admiration for the HM teachers, he notes that, in both private and charter schools, the teachers are the ones who make the real difference in a child's life. He said, "Those students in those charter schools would… could benefit a lot through those educators… through those educators, they start thinking going to college and finishing those, you know, degrees."

Administrator of a Midwestern, HM Charter School Headquarters

The headquarters of the third HM educator I interviewed was in a plaza the size of a large shopping mall in a suburban/business area in the U.S. Midwest.

On arrival, I saw a few cars parked outside. Inside the building, most of the offices looked either vacant or closed, reflecting the economic downturn at the time. I took the stairs to the second floor and walked about a quarter mile-long hallway to get to our appointment. The headquarter entrance consisted of a glass wall with double glass doors. I went inside a small room three times the size of a cubicle to meet my interviewee. The walls were painted in a muted, white color common to such workspaces. The window I sat next to overlook a pond and was the only green view in sight.

Sometimes, the new places I visit remind me of people, events, and places from the past. The headquarters reminded me of Uzbekistan in a peculiar way. However, I found the transparency in the office in stark contrast with the *tedbir* or precaution evidenced in Uzbekistan. I looked back through the glass doors into the translucent atmosphere. Reminding myself that I now live in a democratic country, I took a deep breath and turned on my voice recorder.

The administrator was in his late-30s, with greying hair. He was of average height and weight and dressed very modestly in a clean white shirt with grey pants. The interviewee had worked in a few administrative positions in HM and currently served as the head of a chain of charter schools in the Midwest. A college graduate with teaching experience in HM schools, for the past ten years, he had worked his way up through the network through several administrative positions. The administrator had a very respectful manner and answered my questions diligently. Interestingly, after the interview, he noted he had never heard of the issues related to my inquiry and wanted to learn more. Two themes emerged from our interview: (a) the HM private schools aim to serve all income levels, and (b) the HM educators heavily devote their time and energy heavily to educate their students.

Theme: The HM Private Schools Aim to Serve All Income Levels

The interviewee believed that in the HM philosophy, people are good by nature and "the only way to bring out that good in people is through education." He noted that HM institutions offered quality education while tuition was charged only for school expenses. The administrator emphasized that HM offered scholarships and tuition assistance "to students who are not able to afford them" to reach everybody. He ascertained that "if the schools were able to maintain themselves financially, they would not charge.... tuition."

In general, the interviewee asserted that HM private schools, try to "serve the needs, meet the needs of as many people as possible, many students as possible, or, rich, you know, smart, and mediocre, and different races, and different religions. So, they don't target one specific, you know, population." The interviewee was very confident that HM private schools served as panacea to educational issues of the larger society.

Theme: HM Educators Devote Their Time and Energy Heavily to Educating Their Students.

Like his counterpart, the administrator also strongly believed that the HM educators sacrificed their time and energy to help their students. He noted that HM educators gave up a great deal because "for them this is not only an institutional goal…this is also a personal goal [in] that they see that serving God is serving people.…so they dedicate their life in that philosophy, in that service." The interviewee stated that this dedication inspired HM educators to drive and meet "students to the school on the weekends…[where] they have volunteer teachers from the Turkish community who teach content areas to those students in their own language."

High-Level Executive to Midwestern Educational Organization

This fourth interview took place in a major U.S. midwestern city during the summer. The urban area is famous for their yearly Turkish festival held in a busy business district. I parked my car in a nearby parking garage inside a high-rise building surrounded by glossy windows at all sides. The executive was visiting the festival and requested I join him. Within HM circles, business is often taken care of immediately when a cause arises. Unlike more structured networks, if a person tries to make an appointment, choose a meeting place, and arrange other formalities for an interview, the interchange simply may not happen or will take a very long time to complete. As a result, I needed to be proactive and flexible to conduct the interview and secure data in a public place.

The Turkish festival is a big deal for both the Turkish community and locals who own businesses or celebrate cultural events in the city. As a result, the booths were crowded with media, organizations, and businesses, including national TV networks, the Turkish Department of Tourism, and Turkish

Airlines, a flagship business that sponsored the event. In the future, I learned that the city would host two Turkish festivals so the Zaman newspaper, HM's digital and print media corporation, can lease a spot in public. The venue was extremely jam-packed and sunny with no shade in sight. The executive suggested we meet at a nearby fast-food restaurant on the corner of an intersection surrounded by theaters performing off-Broadway shows.

The interviewee was in his late 30s or early 40s. As a high-level executive in an organization that runs a private HM school, he was married to a Japanese woman. The executive and his wife had two children who spoke Turkish, English, and Japanese. On the day of the interview, he wore a suit and a shirt without a suit jacket. His formal wear on a weekend day reminded me of my past dershane or light house days. Back when I was an undergraduate student, we did not wear jeans and t-shirts. There were two reasons for this: first, HM followers' deep admiration for Mr. Gülen drove us to emulate the father of the movement in similar dress. Second, we were conscious of the importance of *temsil* or representation and understood the need to represent the movement in the best way possible, which included wearing ironed shirts and pants. A single theme emerged from our interview: Hizmet teachers denote quality education.

Theme: Hizmet Teachers Denote Quality Education

The interviewee communicated his high respect and admiration for the teachers and staff working in Hizmet or HM-related schools. He pointed out that Hizmet institutions and schools do not only teach science, math, and other subject disciplines, but strive to develop the moral and spiritual depth of students. In his opinion, the teachers who work in HM schools proved to be the key component. The executive stressed the quality of HM teachers and the way they go above and beyond their limits to help their students, noting: "I see that.... they are spending their days and nights to perform the best education that they can to get ready for [the] classes."

The interviewee also highlighted that HM teachers were ideal role models for their students, possessing high moral qualities, observing "they are not just any people that can teach, but they are people.... who take their cultural values seriously and who try to be good examples for their students." Furthermore, he noted that HM teachers loved their jobs and had a passion for teaching, stating "They are highly responsible educators, men and women, and they, first of all, love the job that they are doing; they love the children."

Interfaith Academic and Professor at HM Institution of Higher Education

For the fifth and final interview, I traveled to a major city in the Midwest to an institution of higher education. In the past, the university was managed by a different Islamic group and operated as an officially recognized, private, not-for-profit, four-year college. However, after their authority to grant two-year and four-year degrees was revoked, the university switched to an unaccredited HM institution offering undergraduate and graduate degrees. The institution also served as a hub for meetings and conferences, and a guesthouse for newcomers or others who need accommodation while visiting the city. While the century-old building was being shared with another private school, plans were in motion for the HM school to take over the entire facility. The modern, ecclesiastical architecture was constructed from brick with a touch of historical accents. The T-shaped structure faced south with long, rectangular windows framed in brick bevels on the first and second floors, while arched windows graced the third floor. From the outside, the windows looked like long, glass surf boards with slightly sharp tips.

I entered the building from a side door and climbed up the stairs to a short hallway with classrooms on both sides. After turning right and descending a second set of stairs, a landing led to a set of double doors, a conference room, and to another hallway. Reaching a narrow door next to an exit, I expected to enter a small room. However, a fully furnished, spacious apartment opened before me facing a large lake. The perimeter of the room was lined with numerous sleeper sofas; a Turkish-styled chandelier hung down from the ceiling. The interviewee and I sat on one of the sofas against the windows to talk.

The professor held a doctoral degree and had been employed at several reputable colleges and universities in the U.S. In addition to teaching in higher education, the elder had chaired an HM organization that focused on interfaith dialogue as a well-known advocate of the movement. The academic was in his mid-fifties, with light skin, blue eyes, and a fuller figure sporting trousers and a shirt. As was the case with all administrators interviewed in this study, the professor was also Turkish. His participation was significant in that he was personally very close with Gülen. A singular theme emerged from our interview, emphasizing that HM teachers are role models for students.

HM Teachers Are Role Models for Students

The interviewee regarded HM teachers as the greatest asset to the schools and the reason behind their pedagogical success. He regarded his fellow educators as the single most important factor in the HM, attesting, "the most important part of the Hizmet schools are the administrators and the teachers. Not only they are good examples for the students, but also, they have very good connections with the families so that they follow the students' behavior, not only in the school borders, but also in the whole life of the student." This distinguished academic underscored the importance of good, available, and accessible role models students could actively emulate, noting: "Teachers and administrators.... the students are taking them as examples in their lives" as they crossed the bridge between the family and the school.

Recommendations and Conclusion

As the saying goes, politics is not education, but education is political. This chapter includes recommendations for HM, take aways, and final thoughts on what has been presented in this book. They are broken into manageable, bite-size sections that can be absorbed as a whole or independent of each other.

Access to Education

On the whole, Gülenian educational philosophy and the HM schools accomplished a great deal in Turkey. Between 1980 and 2000, the first step in obtaining a college education was to pass the Turkish centralized college entrance exams. While the state claimed that high school students should be able to pass the exam based on the public education they received at school, the reality was far different. Additionally, the Turkish economy had a huge demand for college graduates; however, universities did not have enough room to accept large numbers of applicants.

The centralized college exam was an extremely difficult, multiple-choice test at the time. The instrument was not a reliable or valid assessment; the exam failed to measure the knowledge students had learned in school. In fact, the test was designed to limit the number of candidates seeking access to college. The solution to the problem of the test,—or at least to those who could afford it—, was private, after-school college preparation centers. HM joined this educational trend and became very successful, which helped underserved, low socio-economic populations gain access to education and facilitate upward mobility.

HM college preparation centers provided college access to youth from those populations. In the neglected, rural, eastern, and southeastern regions of Turkey, many families cannot afford to provide a decent education for their children despite their desire to do so. HM college preparation centers were opened in these areas under the guise of reading rooms and provided the same quality education to children of those families for free.

Access to Education for Female and Marginalized Students

HM schools helped more girls qualify to obtain a college education in their college preparation centers. Many traditional Turkish families restrict their school-age daughters from having contact with outside world due to parental fear that such exposure may harm them. Families also worry educational institutions will corrupt their female students by teaching and promoting a Western way of life in their curriculum. Also, some conservative families do not want their daughters to have any contact with boys. Thus, after a certain age, parents stop sending girls to school. Both the HM-affiliated private schools and college preparation centers managed to break this tradition by carefully recruiting female teachers and students inviting them into certain branches of the centers and private schools. This was especially important during a time when hijab students were banned from attending classes because of their headscarves.

A New HM Emerges in Exile

As a philosophical construct, HM across the world acts in climates where politicians, stakeholders, actors, and the media have created obstacles to their pedagogical mission. Indeed, traditionalists with strong ties to the past have hindered the academic outreach of Hizmet faculties, schools, and the larger success of the movement's future. Fuller (2014) notes that such roadblocks are often the result of struggle between "democratic Islamism against Muslim autocracy" (p. 6).

In Turkey, after experiencing corruption investigations in 2013 and a failed coup in July of 2016, the relationship between the HM and the JDP government deteriorated. The JDP government engaged in an assault on democracy, confiscating hundreds of schools. The authorities arrested pregnant women, breast-feeding mothers, elderly citizens, and citizens remotely associated with the HM. During this "social and economic genocide" (Hizmet Studies, 2019), the Maarif Foundation Bill was passed with the clear purpose of shutting HM schools. In keeping with the legislation's name translated from the word for "education" in archaic Turkish, traditional Muslims were encouraged to establish their own institutions both domestically and abroad.

The aftermath led to great hardship in Turkey. Members of the HM and other citizens were thrown in jails, tortured, and fired from jobs with rehire restrictions imposed on them by both public and private businesses. Many citizens died crossing the border to Greece; other refugees were abducted abroad by secret services and brought back to Turkey. The steady flow of teachers from Turkey to the United States ceased to a standstill as a result of the persecution. Additionally, HM schools in the U.S. came under fire from the media for hiring non-native teachers. This negative publicity created a shift from employing Turkish, HM-trained teachers to a new generation of teachers working in American HM schools.

The struggle between democratic Islamism and Muslim autocracy gave birth to a new HM, existing today a diasporic community outside of Turkey. As much as it has been a destructive process for many lives, this is also an opportunity to move forward. For example, despite enduring in a state of exile, the contemporary HM does not function as a social justice movement and has not been demanding the return of assets and rights for two reasons: first, HM participants adhere to Gülen's Sufism-oriented teachings in both their educational practices and personal lives; these principles are decidedly neither reactive nor proactive in their aim.

Second, contemporary HM educators hold a deep respect for the state observed by their ancestors for centuries. As the new generation of Muslim citizens of the former Ottoman state, contemporary HM educators regard education as sacred. Historically, the Ottoman king wielded power as both the head of the state and representative of Islam. Although this system was later abandoned, the notion of the Ottoman state is still considered a holy entity in the subconscious of many Turkish citizens to this day.

However, in recent years, peaceful demonstrations have taken place, complaints made to the Court of Justice of the European Union, the UN, and other international organizations. A new social justice and advocacy branch of HM is forming. This is promising for HM as a democratic entity.

Contributing to American Education in a Time of Choice

While the Turkish government's persecution of HM educators was unfolding and the JDP's Maarif Foundation Bill (2016) closed HM schools across the globe, the United States' public school system transitioned from the 2001 Elementary & Secondary Education Act called "No Child Left Behind" to the "Every Student Succeeds Act" (ESSA) passed in 2015. During this time, school choice had allowed HM schools to participate in the American educational landscape as private and charter schools. While challenging ignorance and discrimination, HM schools based on Gülenian educational philosophy proved their merit through their students' academic achievement, garnering medals in national and international science Olympiads. In the present era, some states, including Kentucky, Montana, Nebraska, North Dakota, Vermont, and West Virginia do not permit charter school operations; it will be interesting to see how the HM navigates these policy changes (Thomsen, 2016).

Greater concern must be paid to the latest legal action taken against Harmony Charter Schools in El Paso, Texas, by Amsterdam & Partners LLP, an international law firm backed by the current Turkish government (Source, 2016). The Turkish government has seized HM properties and schools across the globe, diverting funds and resources for its own benefit. In places where private and charter schools are protected by law, the JDP government has sought to obstruct HM school operations through the country's legal system. If this legal challenge should succeed, funding for and by HM schools will be sharply curtailed and a significant number of students from underserved populations will lose access to quality education.

During the 2014–2015 school year, the Harmony Science Academy District enrolled a total K-12 student population of 2,653 (TEA, 2015, p. 13); according to the Texas Education Association, approximately 80% of the district's students were of Latino, Chicano, or Hispanic descent, with 11% from European-American households. African American children represented 6% of the student body, while 1.4% of all students came from families of two or more races. Children of Asian, Native American, and Pacific Islander descent represented 1% or less of the total district enrollment (TEA, 2015, p. 13). Additionally, 74% of the students came from families experiencing poverty. In other words, the district served historically underrepresented and underserved children.

Despite the challenges associated with the violence of poverty, the district met the state's accountability standards and special education requirements in

2015. During the same year, the district also earned a 77% satisfactory standard or above rating in all grades for all subject areas on the State of Texas Assessments of Academic Readiness (STAAR) tests (p. 12). The Turkish government's efforts to close those schools will impede the promising academic growth of the pre-dominantly Hispanic students in these schools.

Charter schools operated by HM educators are the jewels of the crown and should be set apart from their less-progressive counterparts. It is the author's hope that they receive the support and respect they deserve form the American public.

Recommendations for a New Generation of U.S. HM Schools

While HM schools have received the most the attention from sociologists, political scientists, and scholars outside traditional educational circles, future explorations are necessary in education. Indeed, rigorous inquiry could contribute to the larger body of research literature on the interface between philosophy, psychology, and pedagogy, charter schools, and character education.

Intentional Pedagogical Practices and Professional Educational Research

As a result of this study, it became clear that HM schools in the United States possess many ways in which they might improve. My research indicated that HM educators focus on providing quality education via altruistic and equitable practices. All of the interviewees expressed their common goal to help students achieve social, moral, and academic success as exemplary role models for their students.

While this goal aligns with Gülen's philosophy of education, HM educators can venture beyond this sense of altruism to solidify the art and science of their professional pedagogy. For example, I specifically recommend investigations that address how HM educators in the U.S. modify their instruction to accommodate the needs of diverse learners regarding the Common Core State Standards, CCDEI Standards, and WIDA English and Spanish Standards. A case study comparing past and present practices of HM educators' effective strategies for marginalized populations would contribute to the literature, movement, and schools. Qualitative research based on feminist and/or queer theory would additionally be instrumental in determining the role of gender in HM schools.

Scholarly Professional Development in Education and Diversity

HM educators in the U.S. would also greatly benefit from in-depth professional development related to pedagogy, multiculturalism, LGBTQA+ issues, and social justice. Many HM educators in the U.S. hold their first degrees from Turkey; however, most Turkish teacher education programs do not incorporate these topics into preparing teachers; HM educators can become more intentional in their instruction by employing effective practices; they need to plan, apply, and assess instruction based on socio-cultural approaches that build on student background and the individual assets of their students. A comprehensive, articulated explanation of Vygotskian theory and the zone of proximal development would provide a foundation for scaffolding content and language to assist diverse learners in today's classroom.

Curricular Concerns and Considerations

Social studies and arts. On a larger scale, HM schools' historical emphasis on the humanities and "hard" sciences has resulted in providing less attention to the social studies curriculum. Indeed, the lack of attention to the social studies potentially reflects a cultural bias embraced by HM educators and the Turkish Department of Education alike. In 2000–2002, the Turkish public school system reorganized their schools, placing students with lower grade point averages at schools whose curriculums focused on the "soft" or social sciences. On the contrary, top-notch science, psychics, math, biology, and technology teachers were recruited to teach advanced students with high grade point averages in the "hard" or natural sciences.

During my years as an HM teacher in Turkey, Uzbekistan, and Indonesia, I witnessed that the social sciences were left to the management of local educators. In the U.S., Yavuz (2013) suggested HM schools are focusing on science and math while neglecting social studies, arts, humanities, and extra-curricular activities. A chain of HM charter schools school chain in the Midwest prided itself for its focus on science, technology, and math focus in 30+ schools, while dimly noting that subjects such as language arts were taught "as well."

However, across my interactions with the HM's inner circle, I was told several times that Gülen considered this era as the age of the social sciences and the arts. Indeed, Gülen has strongly encouraged HM administrators at the college level to develop art departments and institutions entirely dedicated to the social sciences. As a result, Suleyman Sah University, a completely social sciences institution, was established in 2010 and quickly became the most sought-after private university in Turkey ("Bir bakista," 2013).

Bilingual education. Additionally, HM schools would especially benefit from a clear and concise policy and implementation program for bilingual education. HM educators have established their commitment to diversity, equity, and inclusion; Gülen himself underscored the imperative that individuals sustain their cultural roots by properly learning, protecting, and employing their own mother tongue.

Like many American schools, I observed a lack of teacher and administrator expertise regarding language. Despite a multilingual student population, formal L1 or native and L2 or second language programs had not been established. English as an Additional Language (EAL) classes appeared to be offered on a "need basis" at the discretion of the administrator. By conceptualizing, managing, and enhancing students' linguistic resources, an intentional, systemic, and informed implementation of second language pedagogy could further enhance the mission and goals of HM schools. While some U.S. federal and state policies that do not favor bilingual education programs may be obstructing HM schools from taking steps, nevertheless, educators have a legal, ethical, and moral obligations toward their linguistically rich students.

Non-violent Social Activism. In order to adapt to the demands of democratic societies, HM educators need to make a conscious effort to develop a sense of non-violent social activism for themselves and in the next generation as well. Such action remains essential to carry out Gülen's legacy in the absence of a clear plan for the future. HM educators' next step is to articulate and implement Gülen's thoughts into practice as responsibility they shoulder on behalf of the initiative. In order for Gülenian philosophy to take root, a new corpus of HM educators must be trained. It is commendable that there are steps taken in that direction in the field of education. For example, an HM-related institution, Broken Chalk works "for a better world withstanding against all human rights violations in the educational field" (Brokenchalk, 2020) It is the author's hope that similar initiatives multiply in the near future.

The Future of Gülenian Educational Philosophy and HM Schools

In contemplating the future of Gülenian educational philosophy and HM schools in the United States, there appears to be a shift from establishing K-12 schools in the 1980–1990s to opening universities in the new millennium. Institutions of higher education institutions linked to Hizmet include: Mevlana University in Konya, Nation; Suleyman Sah University in Istanbul, Turkey; Sifa University and Gediz University in Izmir, Nation; Zirve University in Gaziantep, Nation; Qafqaz University in Azerbaijan; the International University of Sarajevo in Bosnia-Herzegova; International Turkmen Turk University in Turkmenistan; Suleyman Demirel University in Kazakhstan; Zaman University in Cambodia; Nile University in Nigeria; Epoka University in Albania; and Ishik University in Erbil, Iraq. All the HM-affiliated universities in Turkey were closed by the AKP regime and are not likely to operate soon. Yet, multiple sources do report that Gülen remains intently interested in the akademisyen hizmeti or academician service.

The HM asserts its existence as an apolitical, educational initiative that derives its strength from high morals and ethics based on the Sufi past of Anatolia. The initiative claims to promote love, peace, and tolerance among all humans regardless of their belief system, race, and ethnicity.

Grounded in such a belief system, the implementation of Gülenian philosophy in teacher preparation and schools has the potential to benefit all levels of the U.S. society. While public education in the U.S. is secular, private, religious schools offer an alternative. For some individuals, religious options are sufficient, while others would like to have more choices. Secular HM universities, private schools, and charter schools staffed by HM educators provide an option for successful institutions based on human universals, devoid of indoctrination. HM educators and schools enforce the morals common to most religions, while equipping students for the future within a non-denominational, humanistic approach. While doing so, they manage to remain secular and sans religious indoctrination. With a proven record of academic success for low-income and minority student populations, HM charter schools have the potential to raise literacy, economic, and health levels, for communities that have traditionally suffered from social neglect, poverty, and violence.

LGBTQA+ and True Outreach

After I broke away from HM over a decade ago, I experienced a wide array of emotions. At times, I held feelings of resentment and felt abandoned by my former co-workers and companions. Other times, I blamed myself, wondering if perhaps if I didn't stick around long enough for the "right" job to appear. Yet ironically, for as much as HM focuses on outreach, I found the culture of HM schools—additionally reflected in the educators' accounts—to be insular: we kept to ourselves. Anywhere I had traveled, I never really integrated nor adapted to local culture(s): there was no need to. I always stayed within my HM circle, which was enough to function. Other HM teachers around me engaged in the same isolated lifestyle.

Therefore, life outside the HM circle was difficult for a while and my time away led to a final realization. I "came out" and identified as a gay, Muslim man. At this point, I am internally questioning the HM's position on LGBTQA+ individuals and my place as a member of that subgroup. Interestingly, Alam (2019) stated in an interview that the HM did not have a conception of "other" individuals because the initiative "did not emerge against somebody" [or anyone] (Hizmet Studies, 2019). He also mentioned that in Germany, many new HM participants he had interviewed would accept an LGBTQA+ family member. On the other hand, HM participants from an older generation were reluctant to embrace non-binary sexual identities, causing me to wonder where the HM situates or makes space for LGBTQA+ members and educators. There is a need for a mindset shift in the HM community. As an LGTBQ+ member, I seek acceptance, not tolerance, from the HM.

Moving Forward

While scholars will be able to draw parallels between Gülenian philosophy and academic literature, I thank the readers of all backgrounds who have tread the complex pathways of this book. My hope is you will see the text as so much more than a research study: it is a story of the education of two men and a nation who came of age during distinct times and desperate places. The narrative attests to the power of kindness, belonging, and thought. This book is in part a personal, in part apedagogical, and in part a philosophical journey of historical-political guideposts; extremes, and exiles; and the intergenerational lighthouses that illuminate the intersecting journeys of our lives. From a Gülenian perspective, all Muslims are brothers and sisters in religion, and all Muslims and non-Muslims are brothers and sisters in humanity. Education stands as a lighthouse to achieve peace through morality and science.

Lastly, there is an old Islamic tale commonly told among Hizmet Movement participants. It is about a man who had committed every sin possible. He eventually realizes his wrongdoings and now wants to redeem himself. He runs into an old wise man and asks if there is any hope for him. The old man tells him he needs a new beginning. He needs "change". To change, the man needs move to a new town. Seeing his chance for a fresh start, he gets on his horse and sprints away. Sadly, he dies before reaching his new town. God asks angels to go measure how far away he was. Was he closer to the new town where he was going to start fresh? Or was he closer to the old place where he had committed the sins? If he had died closer to the new town, he would be granted with heaven; otherwise, he would be going to hell. The angels come down from the sky, measure, and report to God that the place he died was closer to his old town. There is no redemption. He did not make it. He wasn't close to "change." One-way road to hell. Unconvinced, God asks them to go measure again. They try again and surprisingly see this time he was closer to his new town at the time of his death. He was closer to change. They go back and report again. Now there is redemption. Pleased by the new outcome, God forgives the man's sins. The green gates of heaven are now wide open.

A footnote to this tale is that the man was not actually close to the new town. However, since the man tried to "change" in "good faith," had pure intentions in his heart and, since God's compassion superseded his fury, He compensated the difference and shortened the man's distance to his new place.

This is a tale deeply ingrained in the memories of most HM participants. People were assigned and reassigned to different schools, cities, or countries every 2–3 years. While doing so, there was change, a fresh start, to strengthen brotherhood and sisterhood ties. Change indicated progress and letting go of the past. This became a culture within HM. When I look back in time and recollect and muse on my experiences, I admit to the power of change. With change, I shared my space with people from diverse ethnicities, cultural backgrounds, languages, income levels, and people with special needs. HM allowed me to experience the city, the countryside, Central Asia, the Far East, and beyond. I progressed intellectually, culturally and, eventually, made peace with my homosexuality (albeit this may not have been HM's intention).

Today I see an Islamic world that is mostly fractured, compartmentalized, and highly regulated without much room for change and progress. I fear that this will someday reach my doorstep. I fear the society I live in will take a turn around and step back into the dark. Therefore, I believe we need "change" in the right direction. We need progress. There are people who claim that HM has a hidden agenda, is not transparent, and is responsible for the failed coup in Turkey. I am not a political scientist, nor am I a spy; I do not know what happened. I was not there. But my physical, emotional, and mental experiences within HM tell me that HM participants I got acquainted with over the years wanted change and progress for a better world. They all had the best interest of their students, neighbors, friends, and others in mind. It would take a lot more to convince me of such a wrongdoing. And I would like to hear from the conspiracy theorists; "Were you physically there? Did you see it, hear it, feel it, experience it? How do you know what you claim is what really happened?"

This work may have helped the reader empathize with me through my reflections. I recommend my reader pay it forward; Have empathy with HM as well.

APPENDIX A

Translations and/or Transcriptions of Interviewee Responses

Interview Questions and Answers-Participant #1 (Mr. Gülen)

Q1. Share with me your philosophical stance toward education in general, and public versus private education specifically.

The human being, contrary to other creatures, comes to this world as a very poor and needy entity that heavily depends on the help of the others in order to grow and learn. In contrast, an animal, as soon as born into this world, adapts itself. Either in two hours, two days, or two months, it learns the rules of nature, its own relevancy to the environment, and develops the skills it needs to survive. While the human being needs twenty years to develop those survival skills and the various abilities that he needs in order to perform a task, an insect or an animal such as a bee or a sparrow masters it in twenty days, in other words, those skills are revealed to them. Consequently, the animal is not tasked with perfecting itself through education. It is neither tasked with improving itself by mastering a profession. Nor is it tasked with showing its shortcomings, asking for help, and praying. It is exclusively tasked with acting by instinct and exercises its servitude.

The human being enters the world as a needy creature and totally illiterate and unaware of the laws of life. He is so needy that it takes twenty years to learn the living conditions, mayhap till the end of life. He is sent to the world destitute of skills; he hardly learns to walk in one to two years, he learns how to take care of himself in fifteen years, and can only maintain its well-being and avoid damages with the help of modern life.

Thus, the human being, who is born into this temporary guesthouse with a pure nature, has to prove that he deserves to reside in the kingdom of heaven. For that, he must find direction and clarity in thought, in introspection, and in faith; and by fulfilling his servitude, he must progress his heart and soul. Consequently, he must embrace the kingdom of God full of unrevealed secrets in order to understand the secret of existence.

The only means that will lead the human being into divine wisdom and have him serve the common good is education that starts in the family and continues in the society. The child; as a child, may not be able to grasp that the deep meanings that leave a mark in his conscience will, in time, reach even deeper and branch out to other dimensions. Nevertheless, this kind of subliminal acquisition is very important in that those small conceptions will blossom when the time comes and define his character.

However, unless the colors, voices, and utterances we feel during childhood and adolescence are carefully protected, they will vanish into thin air just to be replaced by other things. The child indifferently glances at the beauties and the goodness that form the essence of divine truth. Those beauties should be reworked into the child's mind the same way one would go over a dim writing. Otherwise, they will disappear and won't lead to the fruitful results much hoped for. Yes, unless those feelings, emotions, and thoughts are fed through schooling, consolidated in adolescence, and preserved and protected in one's conscience in adulthood, they will cease to exist even before getting a chance to emerge.

The first and foremost responsibility of a school is to preserve and nurture the seeds of goodness dispersed throughout the spiritual and mental fields of the child's world while weeding out the bad ones. Thus, the good and the beautiful flourishing in the child's subconscious do not get spoiled, nor do seeds of evil grow and inhabit. And thus, the child shall become the builder and representative of feelings coming to him/her in veiled memories and, by making sense of the colors and shapes evolving within and putting together the traces and shadows of the feelings and thoughts he/she indifferently gazed at and was not able to enjoy to the same degree once, he/she will eventually weave his/her own honeycomb of life just like bees hopping on and off the flowers to get honey essence.

It can be said that however perfect the first impressions, observations, and allusions of the child in this alley might be, teachers are the ones who will improve the components of the child's soul and give him/her quality education. It is because of these soul engineers that the child finds his/her own self, aligns his/her thoughts, merges with the culture of his/her ancestors, and sets sail to divine ideals.

The school is the only institution where children are trained to think and work methodologically not only in scientific fields, but also in religious life, national matters and world issues. It is also a place that grooms and flourishes the good and beautiful seeds that first blossomed within the family. Methodological thought and methodological work are crucial fundamentals in science and divine wisdom. Divine wisdom, which means that the mind becomes perceptive to inspiration and is utilized forthright, also proves to be the most venerable and paramount support for religion, morality, and art.

Thus, idealized within this framework, the utmost goal of the school must be to equip them with the highest qualifications, and by doing so to create individuals bound by virtues.

When we look at the issue from such a perspective, the comparison of public and state schools seems superficial. The quality of education may change depending on the country and place. What counts most is to provide quality education, train educators who will provide quality education, and use the resources at a maximum in order to provide the most affordable education to the most number of people.

When the school, environment and the media act together on this shoulder-to-shoulder, then we will have positive and sound results. If one or two of those remain outside this chain, generations will be lost in the midst of an unholy atmosphere created by controversies and differences where conflicts and rivalries abound. It is absolutely imperative that the school be perfect, the family capable, and the environment and neighborhood clean; publications and broadcasts that appeal to the eyes and the ears be supportive of the public conscious and fundamental human values; and, additionally, with control of government when necessary, there be an affirmative and target and direction.

An educational system without a goal and a direction will only confuse new generations, and, when not given enough consideration and thought on what to teach and what methods to follow for their moral education, the same system will turn those generations into nothing more than bellboys of knowledge.

Each individual making up the nation more or less influences others or gets influenced by them. Accordingly, traditions and customs, and someone's inner-outer circle take up an important place in education. Those dealing with the education of new generations, under whatever title that might be, must not even for a split second forget the magnitude and scale of the responsibility they have. We seek all the different ways to guarantee a future for our children, make use of every opportunity, face all hardships to provide them for, and endure all difficulties to give them a heavenly world. Wouldn't all that go into waste if we fail to embed them with their real capital, high morals and divine wisdom; and fail to give them stability with consciousness and culture?

Yes, the best capital is the capital of culture, morality and divine wisdom, and robust willpower flourishing in the bosom of education. Nations that possess such capital own a weapon that can conquer worlds and a secret key that can unlock world's most valuable treasures. On the other hand, those masses unable to lift themselves up to this morality and mentality will get knocked-out and eliminated in the first rounds of their life struggle in the future.

If we manage to equip the minds of young generations with the modern sciences of their times and their hearts with heavenly breezes, and also have them look into the future with lessons from the past like lantern to guide them, believe me, the sacrifices we made to achieve this won't go in vain. On the contrary, we will harvest results in manifold. I can furthermore say that every single penny spent to raise our new generations will turn into a revenue in those dedicated hearts and well-disciplined souls, and will return to us people as a never-ending treasure.

Q2. From your perspective, where does Hizmet's educational institutions rest on this continuum?

A reporter from the New York Times had asked a similar question recently. With your permission, I would rather not call them "Gülen schools," but instead call them private schools founded by non-profit voluntary organizations and follow the state mandated curriculums while delivering instruction.

APPENDIX A

I can say that behind our endeavors in the field of education lies a desire for a peaceful and harmonious world. For years and years, be it in mosques, conference halls, or in my writings, I have stressed the need for a class that is full of love for the living, has great respect to human beings, and is open to live together with others. I encouraged those who found value in what I said to establish educational institutions. I told them that the road to world peace and reconciliation was through the education of new generations that read, contemplated, loved human beings and offered their experiences to their service.

One of the factors that impacted me and made me come to such understanding was this: some years ago while reading Bertrand Russel's "My World View," I stumbled upon a sentence: In response to the question, "If there was a third world war, how would it end?" Russell was saying this: "The deceased will be buried, and the murderer put into jail." This is quite an old comment. However, when we look at the complicated hydrogen bombs and atom bombs today as well as the possibility of different nations capable of using those against each other, we can openly see what he had meant back then. Sadly, it is not possible to take those weapons away from people and destroy them; organizations such as the United Nations can't control that. Consequently, I pondered, "Can we avoid undesired consequences by awakening people into virtues like dialogue, mutual respect, respect for the position of others, and also by coming together around universal values?" and felt an inclination toward educational initiatives. I expressed this feeling both in writing and in my sermons; I tried to channel the public into education. Those who this made a lot of sense to and believed in the importance of such an initiative founded schools in different places; at the moment they still carry on this mission with the same belief, love and enthusiasm.

As for the madrasahs and secular schools: toward the end of their lifespan the madrasahs, in other words a Sufi and mystic lifestyle, shut their doors tight to the positive sciences just as they did to the true Islamic spirit. Eventually, everything except religious teachings was ripped off the madrasahs. They did not take into consideration that not only the Koran, but also ayat-i tekviniye (all creation that shows the existence and oneness of Allah) had to be mastered and used as a structural basis for physics, chemistry, mathematics, and astrophysics. Before myself, scholars like Muallim Cevdet had questioned the deficiencies of the madrasahs. The madrasahs were not able to stand up to the challenge of scientific and technological thoughts and improvements; however, on the other hand, the modern schools could not save themselves from the biases and prejudices of the modernist ideology, either. They couldn't make use of the madrasah experience and knowledge; they followed modernism and neglected the human soul, his/her philosophical and emotional depth, lucidity of thought, spiritual inclinations, and cultural wealth; and they turned into mass production facilities for a global economy.

Were the "Gulen Schools", namely the peoples' schools, able to fill in this void? This is a point of argument. However, in such issues one needs to look at the intent. At the onset of this initiative if the intent was cultivation of the soul and the logic, the marriage of the brain and the heart, and the illumination of the mind and with the light of the heart, then one needs to substitute pure intent with success. That's because in our faith, Allah will reward human beings based on their intent, and treat them as such.

Q3. Several philosophers like Mikhail Bakthin, Paulo Freire, Edward Said, and Lev Vygotsky, among others expressed very different views on education and society, function of schools, and language development of the bilingual child. Their views reflected the needs for educational reform during the times they lived and their ideas were made known to public. Regarding the current times, as well as in the light of educational debates in the near future, what would be an ideal policy for bilingual education?

In a way, we have four thousand years of history as well as a glorious history of one thousand years. We have developed many skills, for example, we have a very sound understanding of aesthetics. It is a duty both for our people and us to display these beauties and open exhibits. Those exhibits today are our educational institutions, schools.

At the end of the day both friends and adversaries appreciate this volunteer movement. This movement is welcomed and appreciated all over the world. However, it does not have a head or a chain of command; it is not organized, neither does it have any recruits. You just talk to people, it makes sense to them, and then they light a torch wherever they themselves are. People say, "We are the offspring of a glorious nation. At one point in history we have coached the world. Why should we confine ourselves into a narrow space and hide in our shell? Why shouldn't we let the world know about us and teach our language? Why shouldn't that beautiful language of ours become the lingua franca? Why shouldn't the foreign emissaries in our country speak Turkish?"

That's what they say and act on it. The Turkish nation has always strived to express him/herself from a different perspective; a perspective and visionary performance only parallel to a nation's fight for independence.

So you saw on TV yesterday; the Afghan ambassador to Turkey was speaking Turkish and was highly praising the Turkish schools in his country. It was also recently on the news that the president of a country called our prime minister and secretary of the state and said, "There are entrepreneurs from Turkey here opening schools; those are our future; please open one or two more here and there."

In sum, the success of Hizmet schools in a world and time where people are extremely polarized; where skin color, ethnicity, and gender inequalities abound, is a result of a work done for the common good and happiness of all human beings. That's why they are very welcomed and accepted in more than 140 countries. The success in those schools is humanitarian.

In addition to these highlighted points, the following factors can be mentioned on why those schools are unique and different from other schools:

We see extreme polarizations in a number of currents as well as in philosophical, political, and social ideologies that emerged in the modern times. There are also pedagogical currents standing at the opposite ends from each other, and cannot save themselves from those philosophical, ideological, and even political polarizations, either. The schools you are asking about may have made it a priority to keep away from such philosophical, ideological, and even political influences, and might have opted for teaching and learning in a common ground without going into the extremes.

Secondly, these schools are welcomed and accepted by people from different geographies, faiths, colors, and ethnicities in every country because they work for the common good of people, prioritize teaching and learning, see that as the most essential part of human existence, and do not intend to use that for any kind of ideological, political, or religious divergence.

Thirdly, no matter what the philosophical arguments about morality, morality determines the basics of the human character. Teachers who work in those schools, hopefully they comply with the moral values at maximum level; may have internalized the universal values and made that second nature to a certain extent. Moreover, those dedicated souls, if they don't see teaching and learning only as a source of income, but as the most dignifying, the most important way and merit that will earn them Allah's blessings and grant them eternal life, and even see it as a form of praying, then they will work without worrying about their work hours and salaries. They will become one with teaching and learning and everything within. Of course, that will make a difference.

Q4. How should different languages be addressed in order to improve the bilingual minority children's school performance?

No child comes to school without any education. The environment influences the human being from the moment he/she is born. The child comes to school being able to speak and with knowledge on many things. The family influences the child between the ages 0–6 more than the school later does and a child's character begins to form in the family.

From this perspective, the goal of education should be to raise spiritually and intellectually developed individuals able to contribute to world peace. This is a crucial point because, as modern pedagogy highlights, lust, anger, greed, and canons of descent affect the individual immensely; for example, even among well-raised young people, albeit less powerfully, those can influence and force them to for down the wrong road. A true human being must not harm anyone and should be a responsible person; he/she has obligations to Allah, his/herself, the society, and the environment. While making use of his/her freedom, the human being may harm him/herself and the others. This is because of his defeat to his nefs (own desires, lusts). That's why we need education; we need to be cultivated. However, schools in these modern times engage with the mind mostly and are regarded as places to train for a job. One's cultivation is not a priority. Therefore they get little attention from the students and the society. However, in addition, schools should also be places where the individual earns his/her hereafter and cultivate them morally, physically, and spiritually. Taking these points into consideration while training them for a job will result in well-qualified individuals. Nowadays, while good schools do offer quality education, they may not be able to cultivate the individual fully. Even access to those schools is very limited and removes equal opportunity. This is the result of a mindset that considers education only for training for a job.

On the other hand, we grew up with yesteryears culture; tomorrow's generations will be the children of the culture of the scholarship we have/will create(d) for them. The present is an extension of the past, and the future is potentially the depth of the present, there is neither a present without a past nor a present without a future.

APPENDIX A

The cultural heritage of a nation inherited from the past is of paramount importance for them. Because of the values and morals from their heritage can they think like themselves, act like themselves, and feel the comfort of being themselves; they will live their lives profoundly and with absolute clarity.

When we consider the issue from the language perspective, language is the most important constituent that defines the human being's vision on how he/she envisions the matter and occurrences. If a nation's language is not strong enough to guard the nation's culture and its value system, then the invasion of that nation's people by other cultures and the loss of their roots in time will be inevitable. They will eventually take on that foreign culture as their own. The human being develops a thought system by reading books, knowledge he/she puts in his mind, and the lexicon he/she possesses. Those familiar with a foreign language, unless they know their mother tongue very well, will ultimately drift into the thoughts of that foreign culture that come from its print or audio-visual means; they will hear like them, think like them, and understand like them. In time, this will cause an inferiority complex and cultural conflicts within the individuals, and will blur their identity. Therefore, one of the imperatives for the individuals to sustain their roots and protect themselves is to properly learn, protect, and use their mother tongue.

Yes, it is very important that children who grow up in a multicultural environment with two languages respect themselves. That is because individuals who respect their own roots and values, and consciously develop their own cultural identity will equally respect the culture of the society they live in and values of other people, and thus, they will live in harmony. Children need to know their mother tongue excellently and possess a language for education very well also so that they can live in peace with their own values, acquire a positively strong personality in the society, can make smooth transitions between cultures without pressure, and lead a serene lifestyle by saving themselves from potential adversities.

Children with a solid first language will learn a second language very well; a child's proficiency in his/her mother tongue will help improve his language of instruction. Children possessing a rich lexicon in the mother tongue will be able to express themselves more easily, will also be able to define words and concepts in the second language more easily, and will learn the language of instruction without difficulty. However, a word of caution is that efforts made only within the family and support provided by the mother and the father is not enough for a child receiving bilingual education to read and write. The society needs to be sensitive and supportive in different ways also;

for example, it needs to develop bilingual education programs for early childhood education.

Additionally, curriculum design should primarily include rhetoric and discourse, ability to elaborate purpose, and ways for self-expression in speech. It is a very sad situation and a destruction of the language when students with 11–12 years of education use words like, "uh, I mean, thing is, er" to fill in the blanks. Teaching composition in remedial classes is not sufficient; students need to take improvisational speech classes. Each student has to be able to present an assignment to his teacher and to the class; then take turns to express his/her opinions on another issue; some other time speak to the public to gain confidence and aptitude; and eventually, upon graduation, he/she should be able to take the stand and address anyone with ease.

Q5. What approach, in your opinion, is the best approach to bilingual education? Where, that is, in which institution (cultural centers, home, schools) should it be taught?

A solid cultural foundation and mind is only possible with proficiency in a language, especially in one's own language. As I pointed out before, if a child develops robustly in terms of culture, namely, if that child learns his/her knows, accepts, and owns his/her core values, in other words-as pedagogy experts would put-, possesses a cultural identity, he/she won't have difficulty in adapting him/herself to a different culture. On one hand, if that child has not sufficiently learned and accepted his/her core values and formed a cultural identity, then he/she will lose self-confidence, fear assimilation and change, and distance him/herself from the culture he/she lives in. On the other hand, if the child is not familiar with the language of the others, and, especially does not speak the language of the dominant culture, then he/she won't be able to communicate his/her needs, and will feel like others are alienating him/her. Moreover he/she will remain an outsider, cannot establish good and profound friendships and end up being alone. It is imperative that children learn the language of instruction in addition to their native language so that they will form a strong personality, their identity will flourish and mold into core values that we call cultural identity, then make positively smooth transitions between different cultures and won't drift away from their own culture nor face psychological issues.

When we look at Turkey, we can say that instruction in a second language and the teaching of a foreign language have not been very successful. That's because instruction in a second language is not as natural as it would be in the first language; it needs a lot of support and use of other means. Unfortunately, this issue has not been resolved in Turkey. As far as I observe, children living abroad cannot learn their first language well enough and do not get sufficient attention from families, schools, and the social environment. Parents and educators need to address this issue with utmost attention and find a method to help children learn their native language as well as the language of the country they live in.

Q6. If it is currently taught, how might the bilingual educational practices be improved? Who should the instructors be? What role and place does bilingual education have and should have in the curriculum?

Even though there are thousands of different languages in the world, the process of learning a language is the same among all human beings; the process is universal. The first teacher of the child is the mother, he/she engages with the sounds and symbols of the language his/her mother speaks the very first time. Children have the skill to learn language at birth; however the environment, family, parents' educational attainment, number of brothers and sisters, and visits and length of stays from extended family members such as grandmothers, grandfathers, and aunts impact language learning greatly. The positive interaction between the child and his/her environment accelerates and enriches his/her language.

In that regard, parents shoulder some responsibilities. The second Khalifa of Islam Hazreti Omar, for example, had pointed out to the value of teaching poetry to children because it fills the heart with love and compassion, and helps them communicate in their language with ease. Also, our heavenly mother Hazreti Aishe, who was reported to have known thousands of verses by heart and spoke beautifully, recommended, "Teach poetry to your children; it sweetens the language."

Thus, parents who want to teach their mother tongue to their children well need to use it exquisitely and ideally in order to set the example to their children. For example, it is unnatural to use words from both languages in one sentence. Researchers say that using Turkish and English in the same sentence with pre-school and elementary school children would harm their mother tongue and education. Parents should talk with their children on each and every subject, choose words carefully, and strive for embedding them into the child's mind, and by repeatedly using the same sentence patterns to naturally teach the grammar of the language.

Especially families that live abroad need to exercise more caution on this. They should read appropriate, interesting, and nicely written books; recite poems and proverbs they would love; and let them watch TV shows that help protect the purity of the language such as Sırlar Dünyası, Büyük Buluşma ve Şubat Soğuğu on Samanyolu TV. On top of these, parents should send their children to their motherland during summer breaks, and have them stay in a decent environment to listen and mingle with people who use the language neatly. At least this would help them familiarize with their language.

Q7. There are charter schools in the U.S. that employ educators and staff with a high regard for Hizmet. What kind of mission are those schools fulfilling in the name of bilingual education?

Firstly, I would like to stress that I am extremely uncomfortable with the phrase "Gulen movement." When people refer to "movement" these days, they refer to a social and mostly to a political trend. You cannot attribute such trends to a poor person like myself. However, if we really, really have to give a name to those activities in order to describe them, and, then we can speak of a "movement." Nevertheless, giving my name to it and calling this movement a "Fethullah Gulen Movement" would be wrong as well as a great injustice to a lot of people. That's because this poor guy has a very limited contribution to it; there is no leadership, headquarter, and neither any affiliation to a command center, or an organization.

At some point in time, you suggest the public to follow some ways; call them to fight against illiteracy, poverty, and secession; encourage them into starting educational initiatives, helping the needy, and aiding victims of disasters wherever in the world that might be. Probably, people with the same mindset value those ideas and consequently there you have a volunteer movement. When those succeed, people in other places in search of such initiatives start doing things in the same line. As a result, you have a service, a form of "market of consent," which solely depends on the voluntary contribution of people with no center, organized structure, by-laws, officiality, and neither needs one. Naturally, some people with high respect to you ask for your advice or you express your ideas either orally or in writing through the means of communication of our times. People, who feel the need to benefit the humankind in their nature, internalize those ideas and come together with others around rationality. Maybe the humane and rational ideas influence those people.

Therefore, attributing all that service to just one person is injustice and blasphemy in our faith. I do not really know how many people are involved in the movement, let alone those who direct many important institutions in different places. I don't know how many countries the service has reached, or how many teachers and students there are. I have been away from Turkey for the past 11–12 years; I can hear the services through the media only. In that regard, even though some call it the "Gulen movement," I call it, at times, the "Service," Movement of Volunteers," and other times "souls dedicated to humankind," or a "Movement in its Own Right." It can also be called, albeit a little long in definition, a "movement of the people who come together around high human values."

The movement, perhaps, has a smiling face as well; welcoming everyone with a smile, open the hearts to everyone; turn the other cheek and not hold any grudge to those who break hearts. These maybe more of the qualities of the movement but they are not small enough to be attributed to just one person. That is a case of a nation professing its character one more time. If we tie all this in with the aforementioned thoughts; this is a movement that would get the consent of people all the way from elite classes to the most illiterate individuals for the sake of controlling the diplomatic conflicts in the world, preventing turmoil, standing against radical positions and behavior, triggering humanly emotions and unearth them, and creating "peace islands" where everyone can live like a human.

The starting point of this lies in the respect for other thoughts, respect for everyone, and coming to an agreement with them through dialogue. The end point is to respect different positions, and, whoever it is, whatever faith or philosophical belief they might have, is to show respect to the individual. Nevertheless, real respect in our religion is the respect to the individual since he/she is a part of Allah's creation. Yes, because humans are Allah's art and creation we respect the person no matter who he/she is. Hazreti Mevlana, with this faith, had called upon seventy-two nations and said, "Come, come, whoever you are come again!" Perhaps our age is a little different; we might do it like this: If you would like to come, please do, our hearts are wide open for you; but wait, don't bother, let us come to you instead. If you will allow us, we would like to come to your country, to your home, just listen to us once; we will listen to you too; you might have beautiful things we might like, you might want some of the beautiful things we have as well; let's get together around a new union on humanistic thought and come up with a new synthesis.

Yes, I only see myself as part of this movement. There might be educators both in private and public schools in the United States who read my books and listen to my sermons on humanism, peace, mutual love and tolerance, co-existence with other cultures, and revitalization of humanistic values. I follow those in press just like everyone else does.

I do not have any idea about the number of those educators. I also do not know the academic excellence of the schools they work at. However, if those schools benefit humanity, and contribute to the love, peace and harmony in the society, then I applaud this. Actually, be it in the field of education or not, I applaud all endeavors that add up to the common values of humanity. I do not discriminate any ethnicity and or religion. This is an essential requirement for being human.

REFERENCES

Abu Huraira (Allah be pleased with him) reported Allah's messenger (2017). https://sunnah.com/urn/240050

AfSV_USA. (2014, January 1). *Evolution of Gulen [Hizmet] Movement with Dr. Alp Aslandogan* [Video]. YouTube. https://www.youtube.com/watch?v=DOkfv_Mc3VA

Alam, A. (2019). *For the sake of Allah: The origin, development, and discourse of the Gulen Movement*. Blue Dome Press.

Alliance for Shared Values. (2016, July 15). *Fethullah Gulen issued the following statement on recent developments in Turkey* [Press release]. http://afsv.org/fethullah-gulen-issued-the-following-statement-on-recent-developments-in-turkey/#.Wb2KPbpFyUk

Amnesty International. (2017). *Amnesty international report 2016/17: The state of the world's human rights*. https://www.amnesty.org/en/documents/pol10/4800/2017/en/

Amsterdam, R. (2022). *Empire of deceit vol II: Web of influence*. Amsterdam & Partners LLP.

Atatürk, M. K. (2014). *Atatürk ilkeleri: Laiklik [Ataturk's principles: Laicism]*. http://www.ata.tsk.tr/04_inkilap/ilkeler.html

Atik, Ö. (2015, September 21). *Gültekin Avcı tutuklandı* [Gultekin Avci arrested]. Hürriyet. http://www.hurriyet.com.tr/gultekin-avci-tutuklandi-30125057

Aymaz, A. (2014, April 20). *Kestane kampi'miz*. Fgulen. https://fgulen.com/tr/basindan-tr/koseyazilari/abdullah-aymaz-zaman-kestane-kampimiz

Basın ve Hakla İlişkiler Müşavirliği. (2017, July 07). *Bakan Bozdağ, Yozgat'ta işyurtları fuarının açılışına katıldı* [Secretary Bozdag attends isyurt fair opening in Yozgat] [Press release].

http://www.basin.adalet.gov.tr/Etkinlik/bakan-bozdagyozgatta-isyurtlari-fuarinin-acilisina-katildi#

Brokenchalk. (2020). *Main.* https://brokenchalk.org/

CBS News. (2012, May 13). *U.S. charter schools tied to powerful Turkish imam* [Video]. YouTube. https://www.youtube.com/watch?v=GJvWP7wBkFs

Çelik, G. R. (2010). *The Gülen Movement: Building social cohesion through dialogue and education.* Eburon Academic Publishers.

Çetin, M. (2010). *The Gülen Movement: Civic service without borders.* Blue Dome Press.

Çetin, M. (2012). *Hizmet: Questions and answers on the Gülen Movement.* New York, NY: Blue Dome Press.

Constitution of the Republic of Turkey. https://global.tbmm.gov.tr/docs/constitution_en.pdf

Daldal, A. (2004). The new middle class as a progressive urban coalition: The 1960 coup d'etat in Turkey. *Turkish Studies, 5*(3), 75–102. https://doi.org/10.1080/1468384042000270335

Demirel, B. (2014, December 14). Gözaltına alınan gazetecilere destek açıklaması [Declaration of support for journalists under custody]. Hürriyet. http://www.hurriyet.com.tr/gozaltina-alinan-gazetecilere-destek-aciklamasi-27771929

Department of Justice Office of Public Affairs. (2016, March 21). *Turkish national arrested for conspiring to evade U.S. sanctions against Iran, money laundering and bank fraud* [Press release]. https://www.justice.gov/opa/pr/turkish-national-arrested-conspiring-evade-us-sanctions-against-iran-money-laundering-and

Dewey, J. (1997). *Experience and education.* Simon & Schuster Inc.

Dialogue Platform. (2015). *Demonizing the Hizmet Movement through media in Turkey: Front covers they don't want you to see.* http://www.dialogueplatform.eu/publications/category/reports

Dönmez, A. (2015, March 31). Mason locası'ndan Y.Şafak'a yalanlama: Gülen üyemiz değil, evraklardaki bilgiler gerçeği yansıtmıyor [Freemasons refute Y.Safak: Gulen not a member, documents inaccurate]. Zaman. http://www.zaman.com.tr/gundem_mason-locasindan-ysafaka-yalanlama-gulen-uyemiz-degil-evraklardaki-bilgiler-gercegi-yansitmiyor_2286350.html

DW Türkçe. (2019, December 24). *Nevşin Mengü ile bire bir: 2019'un ardından* [One on one with Nevsin Mengu: After 2019] [Video]. YouTube. https://youtu.be/fh3qynySNw4

Ebaugh, H. R. (2010). *The Gülen Movement: A sociological analysis of a civic movement rooted in moderate Islam.* Springer.

Erim, N. (1972). The Turkish experience in the light of recent developments. *Middle East Journal, 26*(3), 245–252. www.jstor.org/stable/4324943

European Commission. (2020). *The European Union: What it is and what it does.* https://op.europa.eu/en/publication-detail/-/publication/ac0a88a6-4369-11ea-b81b-01aa75ed71a1

Evren, K. (1980, September 12). Genelkurmay ve milli güvenlik konseyi başkanı orgeneral Kenan Evren'in Türk milletine açıklaması [Chief of staff and head of national security council general Kenan Evren's statement to the Turkish nation][Press release]. https://www.resmigazete.gov.tr/arsiv/17103_1.pdf

Fatih Üniversitesi. (2010, November 23). *General information.* https://web.archive.org/web/20101123094516/http://www.fatih.edu.tr/?genel&language=EN

Fethullah Gülen's life: 1941–1993. (2002, March 09). Fgulen. http://fgulen.com/en/fethullah-gulens-life/about-fethullah-gulen/life-chronology/24903-1941-1993

Flinders, D. J., & Thornton, S. J. (Eds.). (2017). *The curriculum studies reader* (5th ed.). Routledge, Taylor & Francis Group.

Friedman, U. (2016, April 26). The thinnest-skinned president in the world. *The Atlantic*. https://www.theatlantic.com/international/archive/2016/04/turkey-germany-erdogan-boh mermann/479814/

Fuller, G. E. (2014). *Turkey and the Arab Spring: Leadership in the Middle East*. Bozorg Press.

Gage, T. (2014). *Gulen's dialogue on education: A caravansarai of ideas*. Cune Press.

Gülen v. K. H. No. 2000/124. Decision No. 2003/20 (T.C. Ankara 11th High Criminal Court 2006). http://bloximages.chicago2.vip.townnews.com/tucson.com/content/tncms/assets/v3/editorial/a/f2/af27d3fe-6d39-11e0-b666-001cc4c03286/4db211aa9693a.pdf.pdf

GulenMovement. (2012, July 16). *Fethullah Gulen: No return from democracy* [Video]. YouTube. https://www.youtube.com/watch?v=q_GBTbKQOnc

Gündem, M. (2005). *Fethullah Gülen'le 11 gün: Sorularla bir hareketin analizi* [11 days with Fethullah Gulen: An analysis of a movement with questions] (1st ed.). Alfa Basım Yayım Dağıtım Ltd. Şti.

Gürsoy, Y. (2015). Turkish public opinion on the coup allegations: Implications for democratization. *Political Science Quarterly (Wiley-Blackwell)*, *130*(1), 103–132. https://doi.org/10.1002/polq.12287.

Harrington, J. C. (2011). *Wrestling with free speech, religious freedom, and democracy in Turkey: The political trials and times of Fethullah Gülen*. University Press of America.

Harte, J., & Spetalnick, M. (2016, September 25). U.S. network of Turkish cleric facing pressure as those at home seek help. *Reuters*. https://www.reuters.com/article/us-turkey-gulen-usa-insight-idUSKCN11W0BL

Hasanoglu, S. (2012, January 28). *Son Osmanlılar belgeseli 1. bölüm: "Meçhule yolculuk" (Murat Bardakçı)* [The last Ottomans documentary 1st episode: "Journey into the unknown" (Murat Bardakçı)] [Video]. YouTube. https://www.youtube.com/watch?v=_yTQ44LlAZY

Hendrick, J. D. (2013). *Gülen: The ambiguous politics of market Islam in Turkey and the world*. NYU Press.

Hermansen, M. (2015). Who is Fethullah Gulen: An overview of his life. In M. E. Marty (Ed.), *Hizmet means service: Perspectives on an alternative path within Islam* (pp. 18–40). University of California Press.

Hizmet&Anket [@AnketHizmet]. (2019, December 24). *Anket sorusu* [Survey question] [Tweet]. Twitter. https://twitter.com/AnketHizmet/status/1209403067180998656

Hizmet Studies. (2019, December 4). *Hizmet needs to balance reason and faith: Prof Anwar Alam* [Video]. YouTube. https://www.youtube.com/watch?v=0K2B9rMVkeI

International Festival of Language & Culture. (2016). *IFLC is a premier organization for promoting world languages and cultures*. https://intflc.org/

Ipsirli, M. (2003). Medrese: Osmanlı dönemi [Madrasa: Ottoman era]. In *Türkiye Diyanet Vakfı İslam Ansiklopedisi* (Vol. 28, pp. 327–333). Türkiye Diyanet Vakfı İslam Araştırmaları Merkezi.

REFERENCES

İşte Fethullah Gülen'in Masonluk belgeleri. (2015, March 30). *Yeni Şafak Daily*. http://www.yenisafak.com/gundem/iste-fethullah-gulenin-masonluk-belgeleri-2110900

Journalists and Writers Foundation. (1998, July 19). *1st Abant platform meeting addresses Islam and secularism*. http://jwf.org/1st-abant-platform-meeting-addresses-islam-and-secularism/

Kaplan, G., & Öztürk, B. (2015, November 10). *Gülen hakkında 'yakalama emri'* ['Arrest warrant' issued for Gulen]. Anadolu Ajansı. http://aa.com.tr/tr/turkiye/gulen-hakkinda-yakalama-emri/471043

Karakök, T. (2011). Education in Turkey in the Menderes era (1950–1960). *Journal of Higher Education and Science, 1*(2), 89–97.

Karanfil, N. (2015, May 30). *Bank Asya'ya BDDK el koydu* [BDDK seized Bank Asya]. Hürriyet. http://www.hurriyet.com.tr/bank-asya-ya-bddk-el-koydu-29146450

Kazancı, H. (2016, March 04). *Turkey: Trustees enter Zaman HQ under police protection*. Anadolu Ajansı. https://www.aa.com.tr/en/turkey/turkey-trustees-enter-zaman-hq-under-police-protection/531588

Keneş, B. (2020, February 17). Yeni bir Hizmet Hareketi mümkün: Hizmet Hareketi'nin ilkesel/yapısal sorunları ve bir model önerisi [A new Hizmet Movement is possible: The principal/structural issues of Hizmet Movement and a model proposal]. *Blogger*. http://bulentkenes34.blogspot.com/2020/02/yeni-bir-hizmet-hareketi-mumkun.html

Kılıç, B., & Koçak, D. (2015, October 25). *Koza İpek Holding ve şirketlerine kayyum kararı* [Trustee appointment decision to Ipek Holding and its companies]. Anadolu Ajansı. http://aa.com.tr/tr/turkiye/koza-ipek-holding-ve-sirketlerine-kayyum-karari/456215

Kınık, F. (2015, November 27). *Kaynak Holding'le baglantılı 12 şirkete de kayyum atandı* [Trustee appointed to 12 companies afilliated with Kaynak Holding]. Anadolu Ajansı. http://aa.com.tr/tr/turkiye/kaynak-holdingle-baglantili-12-sirkete-de-kayyum-atandi/482303

Koçak, D., & Kılıç, B. (2015, December 17). *Dumanlı hakkında yakalama kararı çıkarıldı* [Arrest warrant issued for Ekrem Dumanlı]. Anadolu Ajansı. http://aa.com.tr/tr/turkiye/dumanli-hakkinda-yakalama-karari-cikarildi/492626

Konda Research and Consultancy. (2016, August). *KONDA barometer: The July 15th coup attempt: August 2016*. https://konda.com.tr/wp-content/uploads/2017/07/KONDA1608_15TH_JULY_COUP_ATTEMPT.pdf

Mijatović, D. (2020). *Country report: Report following her visit to Turkey from 1 to 5 July 2019*. Commissioner for Human Rights of the Council of Europe. https://rm.coe.int/090000168099823e

Moustakas, C. E. (1994). *Phenomenological research methods*. Sage.

Narlı, N. (2000). Civil-military relations in Turkey. *Turkish Studies, 1*(1), 107–127.

North American University. (2020). *NAU history*. https://www.na.edu/about-nau/nau-history/

Nunan, D. (1991). Communicative Tasks and the Language Curriculum. *TESOL Quarterly, 25*(2), 279–295. https://doi.org/10.2307/3587464

Özcan, Z. (2012, June 11). *Önden giden atlıların ilk durağı* [First stop of heralds on horses]. Aksiyon. http://www.aksiyon.com.tr/aksiyon/haber-32793-173-onden-giden-atlilarin-ilk-duragi.html

REFERENCES

Özen, H. (2015). An unfinished grassroots populism: The Gezi Park protests in Turkey and their aftermath. *South European Society and Politics*, 20(4), 533–552. http://dx.doi.org/10.1080/13608746.2015.1099258.

Özer, A. (2008). *Meçhul bir kahraman Mehmet Özyurt* [Unsung hero Mehmet Özyurt]. Işık Yayınları.

Pahl, J. (2019). *Fethullah Gülen: A life of hizmet*. Blue Dome Press.

Pamuk, H. (2015, October 26). *Turkish government hires UK law firm to probe cleric's global network*. Reuters. http://www.reuters.com/article/us-turkey-politics-gulen-idUSKCN0SK20520151026

Pew Research Center. (2016). *Pew-Templeton global religious futures project: Turkey*. http://www.globalreligiousfutures.org/countries/turkey/religious_demography#/?affiliations_religion_id=0&affiliations_year=2020

Said, E. (1980). *Orientalism*. Routledge & Kegan Paul Ltd.

Samanyolu TV. (2017, July 15). In *Wikipedia*. https://tr.wikipedia.org/wiki/Samanyolu_TV

Siegel, R. (Host). (2017, July 11). Cleric accused of plotting Turkish coup attempt: 'I have stood against all coups' [Audio interview]. In *All things considered*. NPR. http://www.npr.org/sections/parallels/2017/07/11/536011222/cleric-accused-of-plotting-turkish-coup-attempt-i-have-stood-against-all-coups

Stockholm Center for Freedom. (2017, July). *15 Temmuz Erdoğan'ın darbesi* [15 July Erdogan's coup]. https://stockholmcf.org/wp-content/uploads/2017/07/15-Temmuz-Erdogan%c4%b1n-darbesi_05.07.2017.pdf

Tachau, F. (2000). Turkish political parties and elections: Half a century of multiparty democracy. *Turkish Studies*, 1(1), 128–148.

Tee, C. (2016). *The Gülen movement in Turkey: The politics of Islam and modernity*. I.B. Tauris.

Tee, C. (2021). The Gülen Movement: Between Turkey and International Exile. In M. A. Upal & C. M. Cusack (Eds.), *Handbook of Islamic sects and movements* (pp. 86–109). Brill. http://www.jstor.org/stable/10.1163/j.ctv1v7zbv8.9

The Eighteenth Brumaire of Louis Bonaparte VII. (n.d.). Marxist.org. https://www.marxists.org/archive/marx/works/1852/18th-brumaire/ch07.htm

The Global Entrepreneurship Network. (2021). *Kaynak Holding*. https://www.genglobal.org/kaynak-holding

The Maarif Foundation. (2023aa). *Establishment purpose*. https://turkiyemaarif.org/page/about-us

The Maarif Foundation. (2023b). *Minister of National Education Ismet Yılmaz met with the ambassadors of African countries* https://turkiyemaarif.org/news/minister-of-national-education-ismet-yilmaz-met-with-the-ambassadors-of-african-countries

Tüfekyapan, A. K. (2017, May 26). *Başvekil Adnan Menderes (Ahaber)* [Prime minister Adnan Menderes (Anews)] [Video]. YouTube. https://www.youtube.com/watch?v=CNDYfCTEGko

Usta, A. (2015, May 01). *Hakim Metin Özçelik'in ardından Mustafa Başer de tutuklandı* [Mustafa Baser arrested after judge Metin Ozcelik]. Hürriyet. http://www.hurriyet.com.tr/hakim-metin-ozcelikin-ardindan-mustafa-baser-de-tutuklandi-28882854

Van Manen, M. (2014). *Phenomenology of practice: Meaning-making in phenomenological research and writing*. Left Coast Press, Inc.

Vygotsky, L. S. (1978). *Mind in society: The development of higher psychological processes* (M. Cole, V. John-Steiner, S. Scribner, & E. Souberman, Eds.). Harvard University Press.

Weller, P. (2022). *Hizmet in transitions: European developments of a Turkish Muslim-inspired movement*. Palgrave Macmillan.

Yavuz, H. (2013). *Toward an Islamic enlightenment: The Gulen movement*. Oxford University Press.

Yılmaz, İ. (2015). *Kemalizm'den Erdoğanizm'e* [From Kemalizm to Erdoğanizm]. Ufuk Yayınları.

www.ingramcontent.com/pod-product-compliance
Lightning Source LLC
Chambersburg PA
CBHW061720300426
44115CB00014B/2762